"Reading this elegant biography will make those of us who knew Father Ted miss him all the more, and those that never met him wish they had. Hesburgh's unparalleled ability to build bridges across polarizing divides, so richly described by Hahnenberg, should prompt contemporary Americans both to admire his legacy—and to emulate his approach."

—Kathleen Sprows Cummings
   Professor of American Studies and History
   University of Notre Dame

"Theodore M. Hesburgh, CSC, helped make Notre Dame a great Catholic university and a great American university. He did that life work as a priest and citizen, and he inspired generations of Catholics to keep their faith precisely by doing excellent work. Edward Hahnenberg tells Hesburgh's rich story as a man of the center, mediating differences and seeking common ground and common goods. This book will help us to recover something of Father Ted's hopeful American and Christian faith in God and one another."

—David J. O' Brien
   Professor Emeritus
   College of the Holy Cross

"Edward Hahnenberg tells the amazing story of the University of Notre Dame's legendary president, whose life and times encapsulate some of the most remarkable transformations, which the twentieth century wrought in universities, the Catholic Church, America, and the world. In this telling of Hesburgh's life, the priestly vocation of a six-year-old boy finds expression in Father Ted's dedic   ministry as mediator and bridge builder. Grounded in h celebrating Mass, he addressed contemporary challeng rights to student protests to nuclear war with an optim his faith in Christ and the goodness of humanity."

—Sandra Yocum, University Professor of Faith and
   University of Dayton

People of God

Remarkable Lives, Heroes of Faith

People of God is a series of inspiring biographies for the general reader. Each volume offers a compelling and honest narrative of the life of an important twentieth- or twenty-first-century Catholic. Some living and some now deceased, each of these women and men has known challenges and weaknesses familiar to most of us but responded to them in ways that call us to our own forms of heroism. Each offers a credible and concrete witness of faith, hope, and love to people of our own day.

John XXIII by Massimo Faggioli

Oscar Romero by Kevin Clarke

Thomas Merton by Michael W. Higgins

Francis by Michael Collins

Flannery O'Connor by Angela O'Donnell

Martin Sheen by Rose Pacatte

Dorothy Day by Patrick Jordan

Luis Antonio Tagle by Cindy Wooden

Joseph Bernardin by Steven P. Millies

Corita Kent by Rose Pacatte

Daniel Rudd by Gary B. Agee

Helen Prejean by Joyce Duriga

Paul VI by Michael Collins

Thea Bowman by Maurice J. Nutt

Shahbaz Bhatti by John L. Allen Jr.

Rutilio Grande by Rhina Guidos

Elizabeth Johnson by Heidi Schlumpf

Augustus Tolton by Joyce Duriga

Paul Farmer by Jennie Weiss Block

Rosemary Nyirumbe by María Ruiz Scaperlanda

James Martin, SJ, by Jon M. Sweeney

More titles to follow . . .

Theodore Hesburgh, CSC

Bridge Builder

Edward P. Hahnenberg

LITURGICAL PRESS
Collegeville, Minnesota

www.litpress.org

Cover design by Red+Company. Cover illustration by Philip Bannister.

© 2020 by Edward P. Hahnenberg

| 1 | 2 | 3 | 4 | 5 | 6 | 7 | 8 | 9 |

Library of Congress Control Number: 2020930305

ISBN 978-0-8146-6458-2   978-0-8146-6482-7 (e-book)

For my Notre Dame professors, with gratitude

Contents

Preface

As this manuscript neared completion, two major contributions to the narrative history of Father Theodore M. Hesburgh, CSC (1917–2015), appeared—and they could not have been more different. The first was a 104-minute documentary, *Hesburgh*, produced by Christine O'Malley and Jerry Barca, and directed by Patrick Creadon. The second was a 442-page biography, *American Priest: The Ambitious Life and Conflicted Legacy of Notre Dame's Father Ted Hesburgh*, written by Notre Dame history professor and Holy Cross priest Father Wilson Miscamble, CSC. Both attempt a comprehensive overview of Hesburgh's life. Both leverage interviews and extensive research. Both draw on many of the same primary and secondary sources. Yet their tone and conclusions differ markedly. The documentary celebrates Hesburgh as a civil-rights hero, a visionary leader, and a consistent moral voice in tumultuous times—the conscience of a nation. Miscamble's biography paints a less flattering portrait, downplaying Hesburgh's influence and portraying him as a tool of the secular liberal establishment—"the accommodating and acceptable priest."[1]

These recent works have sparked wide-ranging commentary, suggesting a renewed interest in the fascinating figure of Father Ted. Responses run the gamut, as the assessment of Hesburgh's legacy often becomes a proxy for larger debates about where church and society are headed. Unfortunately, such debate can stir up the toxic polarization that poisons so much of our public discourse. At the same time, it can bring to the surface a deep desire for the kind of leadership capable of overcoming such divisions, the kind of leadership that Hesburgh himself embodied.

Father Ted certainly had his flaws. He was not always a prophet. But he was not a partisan. And he was never a pawn. In this, O'Malley and Barca's documentary comes closer to the truth than does Miscamble's biography. In particular, the film's attention to Hesburgh's work as a mediator—a bridge builder who engaged people on all sides of an issue—captures the essence of Hesburgh's self-understanding and sense of purpose. As the journalist Ted Koppel, interviewed in the film, put it: "What made [Hesburgh] such an extraordinary figure was that he didn't really belong to any side. He belonged to the side of decency. He belonged to the side of a fundamental belief in the redeemability of mankind."[2]

The following story offers an introduction to the life of a priest who worked hard to bring people together. Like *Hesburgh* and *American Priest*, my more modest contribution relies on the prior research and careful records of a well-documented life. In the archives at the University of Notre Dame, Hesburgh's papers fill boxes that extend over 518 linear feet—not to mention extensive video, audio, and digital holdings that record over six decades of activity both on and off campus. My sincere thanks go out to the archive staff for helping me navigate this material and, in particular, to W. Kevin Cawley and Joe Smith for their concrete assistance. Two awards (2016, 2019) from Notre Dame's Cushwa Center for the Study of American Catholicism helped cover travel expenses for research. I want to thank Kathleen Sprows Cummings, Director of the Cushwa Center, for her support and insight.

Over the course of his career, Hesburgh wrote hundreds of essays, articles, and speeches and published five books. He was featured in dozens of magazine and newspaper articles and has been the subject of several biographies. Many of these writings appear in the notes and bibliography below. Two books proved to be indispensable in offering an orientation to Hesburgh's life. The first is Hesburgh's own best-selling autobiography, *God, Country, Notre Dame*, written with Jerry Reedy (1990). The second is Michael O'Brien's comprehensive volume, *Hesburgh: A Biography* (1998). I am indebted to these earlier narratives, as well as to the work of Charlotte Ames, Joel Connelly and Howard Dooley, John Lungren, Robert Schmuhl, and Thomas Stritch. In their biographies, the basic plot of Hesburgh's life plays out. What I hope to add is more insight into the main character of this story, and to do so by exploring the spirituality that sustained and inspired Father Ted.

I am grateful to Father John Jenkins, CSC, for first introducing me to Father Hesburgh, and to Fathers Richard McBrien and Thomas O'Meara, OP, for sharing so many stories. Thanks to Kathleen Sprows Cummings, Bob Krieg, Ed Mish, Paul Murphy, and Sandra Yocum for feedback and encouragement on the manuscript. And thanks to Shannon Chisholm, Hans Christoffersen, Peter Dwyer, Michelle Verkuilen, Stephanie Lancour, Nancy de Flon, and the whole team at Liturgical Press for transforming it into a book. Finally, my deepest thanks go to Julie, Kate, Meg, and Abby for . . . well . . . everything.

Introduction

There is no passivity in his contemplation, since the realization of God's will demands that the person throw all of himself into the cause. There is no gloom in his dedication, since it is sustained by a confidence that the Holy Spirit is at work in us all, in the world, and in the cosmos.

—Kingman Brewster, Jr.[1]

Anyone who ever met Father Ted Hesburgh walked away with a story. Here's mine.

When I was a graduate student at the University of Notre Dame, I had a small office on the twelfth floor of the library—a building named after Father Ted but better known as "Touchdown Jesus" for its huge mural of Christ looking out over the football stadium.

The office was small, just big enough for a desk. But it had a spectacular view of campus. It was the same view, I bragged to my friends, that Father Hesburgh had, whose much larger office was directly above my own.

Hesburgh had stepped down as university president several years earlier. During his thirty-five-year tenure he had become a national leader in civil rights, public policy, and education. He had advised popes and presidents, served on countless commissions and boards, and even earned the world record for the most honorary degrees received. Thus retirement was something of a relative term for Father Hesburgh. Well into his eighties, he still went into the office every day. And one of the best things about my time on the twelfth floor was that I often got to share the elevator with Father Ted.

Hesburgh loved to talk to students. Whenever students got on the elevator, he immediately asked what they were studying. When they said physics or history, Hesburgh would share some anecdote about his work on the Atomic Energy Commission or the time he marched with Martin Luther King, Jr.

Over the months we rode the elevator together, I had the same conversation with Father Hesburgh three times.

Every time, the conversation began with his question, "What are you studying today?"

And every time, I responded, "I'm working on my dissertation in theology."

"*Really?*" he said, clearly not remembering our previous chats. "You know *my* doctorate was in theology. What's the topic?"

"I'm writing on lay ministry in the Catholic Church," I replied.

"*Really?*" Hesburgh said, as he looked up at me with new interest. "*My* dissertation was about the laity."

"I know, Father," I honestly answered, "I've read it. It's very good."

"Well, in those days, a dissertation on the laity was controversial," he went on. "This was the early 1940s, remember. My advisor told me not to do it. He wanted me to pick another topic. But I knew it was too important. And so I pushed ahead."

"That doesn't surprise me, Father," I said, smiling.

"I finished the dissertation and got it published. Soon after, I received a letter from the Holy Office in Rome. They wanted me to send them a copy for review. I thought for sure I was going to be censured. It used to be called the Holy Office *of the Inquisition*, you know. In the end, I dutifully sent in the volume, and that was the end of it. I never heard back."

He continued, "Eventually the pope died, and the cardinals elected John XXIII, who surprised everybody by calling a Second Vatican Council. And what do you know was on the agenda? The laity! The council dedicated a whole document to the laity!"

Then came the punch line.

"I'll never forget reading that document when it first came out," Father Hesburgh deadpanned, "they stole all my ideas."

This was a story that Hesburgh clearly loved to tell. Since those elevator rides, I've heard a number of his friends share some version of it. No doubt it got better over time. Hesburgh was the first to admit that one of the things he inherited from his Irish mother was a tendency to exaggerate or embellish stories—"piling it," his father would say. So it may be too much to conclude that Hesburgh was the unknowing ghostwriter of Vatican II's Decree on the Lay Apostolate. Still, his choice of a dissertation topic was prescient. His early interest in the active role of the laity anticipated themes that would burst out decades later at the council. Here we catch a glimpse of the young Hesburgh, already alive to new ideas and quick to see their practical implications.

The narrative that follows is an invitation to get to know a remarkable person. Father Ted was a towering figure—a

giant of twentieth-century American Catholicism. It is hard
to exaggerate the impact he had on the academy, the church,
and the broader society. A charter member (and later chair)
of the US Civil Rights Commission, Hesburgh accepted
sixteen presidential appointments over the course of his life.
He worked on racial justice, nuclear nonproliferation, Third
World development, immigration reform, international humanitarian aid, ecumenical dialogue, educational policy, and
a host of other social issues—in addition to leading the
University of Notre Dame through three and a half decades
of extraordinary upheaval and unprecedented growth. The
man left his mark.

In telling Hesburgh's story, however, I am less interested
in charting his legacy or assessing his influence. Instead, I
hope to introduce the man himself. I want to know Father
Ted Hesburgh as a real human person, in order to lift him
up as a compelling and credible witness of Christian dis-
cipleship in the world today.

In getting to know Hesburgh, the biographer faces a
special challenge. Although Hesburgh was a prodigious
storyteller, he was not particularly effusive in describing his
own inner life. This is not the sign of a superficial personal-
ity or a shallow spirituality—far from it! Hesburgh's generous intellect, his courage in the face of obstacles, his
compassion toward those who suffer, and his many close
and loving friendships point instead to great depth of character. His complete trust in the work of the Holy Spirit and
his dependable devotion to prayer indicate a profound relationship with God. Perhaps the reason Hesburgh spoke
so little about his own inner life was because he embodied
an activist spirituality, preferring ministry over contemplation, service to others over consideration of the self. Perhaps
it was because he never suffered from a serious crisis of

faith—the "dark night of the soul" that so often illuminates spiritual autobiography. Perhaps it was because, as one fellow Holy Cross priest who knew him well put it, "he just wasn't a complicated guy." Hesburgh's faith was simple, straightforward, and strong. The following story is based on the premise that we can get to know this faith—and thus get to know Hesburgh—by understanding the convictions that animated his life, convictions that are revealed in his words and in his deeds.

Of those convictions, none was more important than his own sense of calling. When asked what he would put on his tombstone, Hesburgh did not hesitate. It would be one word: *Priest*. From the age of six to the day he died, Hesburgh knew that he was called to be a priest. For all his accomplishments, what is most striking in the stories told about Hesburgh are the countless acts of priestly ministry that people remember—a hospital visit out of the blue, a prayer card sent with his condolences, a handwritten note of encouragement, a late-night counseling session, an intimate Mass celebrated in a living room, at a nursing home, or on the edge of a barrio. His one-time provost Nathan Hatch observed, "He never seemed to doubt who he was and was thus free to relate to people as they were—no condescension, no putting on airs."[2] Hatch then recalled a story of Hesburgh blessing his pregnant wife and child—a gesture that the couple, who are not Catholic, found warm and welcoming. Hesburgh was a university president and committee chairman who often behaved like a small-town pastor. "Each time I am called 'Father,'" he wrote in his autobiography, "I know that the caller owns me, as a child does a parent, and that he or she has a call on me for anything needed, especially compassion and understanding in the spirit of Christian love."[3]

To be a priest meant something more to Hesburgh than being a pastor. It also meant being a *mediator*. To be a mediator is to stand in the middle (*medium*) between two separated realities in order to span the gap, to unite what is apart. Hesburgh, who was trained in the hairsplitting distinctions of neoscholastic theology, knew that Saint Thomas Aquinas defined the priest as a mediator—a bridge (*pons*) between God and humanity. The ultimate mediator, of course, is Jesus Christ, the great high priest, who in his very person united humanity and divinity and who, through his death and resurrection, reconciled the world to God. The ordained priest participates in the priesthood of Christ, and thus the central purpose of his ministry is to continue Jesus' work of bridge building. "The priest tries to bring God's word and grace to humankind and strives as well to bring humankind to God, in faith, hope, and love."[4] But being a mediator is not solely the prerogative of the ordained. This was the great lesson Hesburgh learned from his doctoral dissertation. Every baptized Christian participates in Christ's priesthood in his or her own way. The laity, as well as the clergy, are called to be bridge builders. All are called into the breach, to overcome divisions and draw people together.

Hesburgh always placed himself squarely "in the middle." He always sought to mediate. According to Hatch, Hesburgh could not be put in a conservative or liberal box. "He clung to virtues on both sides of many modern debates. He was a huge champion of ROTC at Notre Dame and, at the same time, he championed peace studies. . . . He was friend of the Rockefeller brothers and of Martin Luther King Jr., confidant of Republican and Democratic presidents, champion of the Catholic character of a place like Notre Dame and of intellectual freedom and institutional independence."[5] Hesburgh's special charism was his ability to combine strong conviction with grace and generosity to all. In our own polarized time, such saints of the center are in short supply. If there is a thesis in what follows, a slant I give to the story, it is this: Father Hesburgh is worthy of our attention because he models the kind of bridge building that our world needs now more than ever before.

CHAPTER ONE

Faith in the Family

When Ted Hesburgh was in the eighth grade, four Holy Cross priests visited Syracuse, New York, to preach a mission at his parish church, Most Holy Rosary. An altar boy at the time, Ted struck up a conversation with the friendly priests. When one of them, Father Tom Duffy, asked the boy what he wanted to be when he grew up, Ted replied with conviction, "I'm going to be a priest, Father. Like you."[1]

Impressed, Father Duffy jotted down Ted's name with a note ("fine boy, bright"), and later called on his parents to encourage them to enroll Ted in the high school seminary run by Holy Cross at the University of Notre Dame. Ted's mother, who knew he had always wanted to be a priest, worried that he was too young to leave home. Father Duffy urged her, "If he doesn't come and he goes to high school here, he may lose his vocation." To this misplaced concern, Anne Hesburgh replied firmly, "It can't be much of a vocation if he's going to lose it by living in a Christian family!"[2]

Four years later, Anne, her husband Theodore, and their two oldest children, Mary and Ted, piled into a borrowed Hudson Essex for the six-hundred-mile drive to South Bend,

Indiana, where Ted would start classes at Notre Dame as a Holy Cross seminarian. As soon as he had said his goodbyes, Ted was overwhelmed with homesickness. "For one month I never unlocked my trunk because I didn't know whether I'd stay." Eventually, the gloom lifted as Ted settled into the routine of seminary life. But years later he remembered those first weeks away from home as a very difficult time. "Maybe that was the price I paid for having a good family."[3]

It was, by all accounts, a good family. In addition to an older sister, Mary, who was particularly close to Ted, there were two younger sisters, Elizabeth (Betty) and Anne. For years Ted prayed for a brother, and he had just about given up hope when, at age sixteen, the prayer was answered. James, or Jimmy as they called him, was only nine months old when Ted left for Notre Dame—leaving it to later in life for the two brothers to become good friends.

Ted's mother and father were a study in contrasts. His father was German, taciturn and sober, a serious business-man who took great satisfaction in his family and his work. "He felt deeply," Betty later reflected, "but he never quite let you know."[4] The man read extensively, obsessed over crossword puzzles, and loved drubbing his children at Scrabble. Shortly after the younger Ted became president of Notre Dame, his father beat him once again at the game, wryly commenting, "They just don't make college presidents the way they used to."[5] Ted's mother, born Anne Marie Murphy, was Irish through and through. "An aura of joy and merriment seemed to surround her all the time."[6] She laughed and sang often and loved being with people. She also loved to travel and dreamed of living in New York City in order to enjoy its theater, opera, and culture. Her husband, who got his start as a traveling salesman, hated the city and wanted nothing more than a quiet night at home with a good book. Ted thought his parents complemented each other well and appreciated what he inherited from each. "My German side gave me a sense of order and discipline; my Irish side gave me the ability to understand people [and to] get along with them."[7]

Ted Hesburgh described his childhood as a normal one. Born on May 25, 1917 (four days before the birth of John F. Kennedy, he liked to point out), Theodore Martin Hesburgh grew up through the boom and bust of America between the two world wars. When Ted was eight years old, his father—by then a manager for the Pittsburgh Plate Glass Company—moved the family out of their apartment into a new two-story, three-bedroom colonial on the edge of Onondaga Park in the Stratmore section of Syracuse. The children enjoyed sledding, skiing, and skating in the winter. In the summer, the family would picnic on the weekends and spend two weeks every year at a cottage on Lake Ontario. As the Depression set in, Ted's father kept his job, but money was tight. The eldest son helped out by cutting grass, hauling coal ashes, and delivering newspapers. By his senior year in high school, Ted was working forty hours a week at the local gas station.

Ted was a Boy Scout who built crystal radio sets and model airplanes—developing an early interest in aviation, which was only heightened by a short ride in an open-cockpit barnstormer when he was ten. He was a voracious reader, devouring all kinds of literature—especially stories of adventure, romance, and travel. He loved tales of heroic priests, such as Father Bernard Rosecrans Hubbard's *Mush, You Malamutes!*, about a missionary in Alaska. In an editorial he wrote for the school newspaper in his senior year, Ted challenged his classmates to raise the bar in their own literary pursuits. Drop the stupid "dime novels," he exhorted, and start reading books "that will elevate your ideas, enlarge your vocabulary, and widen your perspective."[8] Ted dabbled in sports, playing baseball and serving a brief stint as lineman on the neighborhood football team ("I wasn't very good"), but he never developed an interest like that of his father, who was an avid sports fan. Ted did love to hunt and fish—so much so that, during his senior year, the star student skipped classes on the first day of pheasant-hunting season. It may have been the only time he ever got in trouble with his teachers.[9]

The center of this happy childhood was Most Holy Rosary School, which Ted attended for twelve years. Most Holy Rosary Parish was founded in 1913 and immediately put up the school, before it had even begun construction on the church. Ted grew up going to Sunday Mass with his family in the school auditorium. The Roaring Twenties had fueled the ambitions of the founding pastor, Father George Mahon. When the Depression hit, his plans remained unfinished and his bills remained unpaid, leaving the parish half a million dollars in debt. Ted remembered how weary he grew of the constant plea from the pulpit for more donations. "All we heard about was money."[10] In fact, one of the things that attracted young Ted Hesburgh to a religious order rather than the diocesan priesthood was—irony of ironies for the future college president—the thought that he would never have to do any fundraising!

The genius of the Catholic schools of that era was the way they served as a hub for the whole of Catholic life. Families revolve around the children, which means they revolve around the school. This was certainly true for Most Holy Rosary and for the Hesburghs. All of the children attended Holy Rosary from first grade through high school. There, and at home, they were encouraged to be "religious." They never missed Mass, never ate meat on Fridays, and often prayed the rosary together as a family. Ted did his best to avoid lying, stealing, cheating, and a whole list of other sins. "And we never, never talked about sex—in any way, shape, or form."[11] When he fell short, there was always confession and the regular grace of the sacraments.

In a time of widespread religiosity, Catholics still stood out. To their Protestant neighbors, Catholics seemed clannish and odd, even a little suspicious. They clustered in immigrant enclaves. They established separate schools (and hospitals and credit unions and clubs) and had large families. They worshiped in an ancient language, filled their churches with statues of strange saints, followed the direction of celibate priests and enigmatic nuns in peculiar clothing, and gave their allegiance to a foreign authority in Rome. In return, Catholics—convinced that theirs was the "one true church"—looked out on the world with their own suspicions. Daniel J. Curley, the bishop of Syracuse when Ted was in grade school, urged Catholics not to associate with non-Catholics. "We are bound to regard all other conceptions of God as false, an insult to his divine majesty." In a 1930 pastoral letter, Curley railed against the "pagan morality" of contemporary society, condemning, among other things, the "putrid stream" of lewd literature and pictures that were "debauching the minds and morals of the young." He denounced the "neo-paganism of birth control," which was based on a degrading self-indulgence that led to "a lustful perversion of the marital relationship" and the "prostitution of motherhood."[12]

To protect themselves from such threats, seemingly coming from all sides, immigrant Catholics in places like Syracuse had worked hard to build up a parallel set of institutions, which kept outsiders at bay and sustained a distinctive Catholic culture in the midst of Protestant America. Ted's childhood was happy but homogenous. Growing up in Syracuse, he never knew a black person. He knew very few people who were not Catholic. He had a vague idea, for example, that Jews were "somewhat different" and that being different was a "bad thing." As an adult, Hesburgh admitted that his thinking as a child was something like this: "They're not like us. . . . Why can't everybody be like us?"[13]

Ted enjoyed a kind of privileged innocence that was complicated one afternoon when he arrived home from grade school to find his mother comforting a neighbor woman sobbing in their living room. Embarrassed, Ted slipped into the kitchen to make a sandwich and later asked his mother what happened. His mother explained that the woman was Jewish, that she had lived down the street for two or three years, and, in all that time, Ted's mother was the only one who had ever talked to her. Unable to take it anymore, the woman had finally decided to move away and had stopped in to say goodbye. Ted didn't understand, so his mother explained that they lived in a segregated neighborhood— almost completely Protestant, with just a few Catholics and no other Jewish families. The only reason the Catholics were tolerated, his mother said, was because they had a little money. When Ted asked his mother why she had befriended this woman, Anne replied, "I talked to her because I grew up in New York. In our building, we had Jews on the right and Jews on the left, Jews upstairs and Jews downstairs. . . . We learned to understand each other, and we supported each other. Otherwise, we would have gone down the drain together. There's no way on earth I could be prejudiced against Jews."[14] It wasn't an earth-shattering revelation, but Ted never forgot his mother's words.

If the downside of the Catholicism of Ted's youth was its tendency to look inward, to circle the wagons, to condemn "the world" beyond its walls, the upside was its ability to foster community, a sense of belonging, and a thick religious identity. In his impressive history of the Diocese of Syracuse, David O'Brien observed, "The Church, then, was a source of truth and grace and at the same time a set of associations, family, friends, companions."[15] Clearly this world was the soil that nurtured Ted's vocation. "I *always* wanted to be a priest," he claimed.[16] There was simply no higher calling, no more challenging, more rewarding life than that of a priest. If Theodore and Anne had hoped their son would pursue such a path, it doesn't seem to be something they pressed upon him. They didn't have to. It was in the air. Indeed, for its thirtieth anniversary in 1943, Most Holy Rosary School boasted that thirty-six of its graduates had become priests and twenty-eight more were vowed religious.

For Ted, the thought of becoming a priest—of standing between God and humanity, with the "traffic going both ways"—was romantic and adventurous.[17] Throughout high school, Ted dated and danced, attended parties, and stayed out late with friends. During his junior and senior years, he spent a good deal of time with one classmate in particular, Mary Eleanor Kelley, who thought the world of him. But Ted felt called to something more than an active social life. And everybody knew it. When the high school put on a production of Christ's passion, titled the "Mysteries of the Mass," two hundred students took part. Ted played the lead, earning accolades in the local Catholic press. The review, which singled out Ted's portrayal of Jesus as "particularly commendable," described the play as a "magnificent religious spectacle . . . So dramatic was the performance that it thrilled the hushed throng for nearly three hours." "You would think he was Christ!" recalled a classmate. "He *was* the play. After the play, everybody thought for sure he would [enter the priesthood]."[18] When the class of 1934 compiled their predictions about where each of the graduating seniors would be in ten years, they pegged Ted: "Pastor of St. Peter's in Split Rock."

Hesburgh never made it to Split Rock. Instead, he slung south along the shores of the Great Lakes Ontario and Erie to the flat cornfields of northern Indiana. In mid-September of 1934, Ted fulfilled "the dream of practically every Catholic schoolboy in the country" and enrolled at Notre Dame.[19] That first year, he lived and took most of his classes at Holy Cross Seminary (later Holy Cross Hall), a stone's throw from the impressive neo-Gothic Church of the Sacred Heart and its famous grotto. Though technically Notre Dame students, the seminarians had little to do with campus life. Indeed, they had little to do with anyone other than their fellow seminarians and their priest-professors. No dating. No clubs. No letters to old girlfriends. No trips home for Christmas.

Hesburgh threw himself into his studies. Alongside compulsory courses, he signed up for extra electives in Latin and Greek. He tolerated his science classes and enjoyed studying philosophy, literature, and languages. He fashioned himself a strong student, and he was. However, on one "A" paper, his professor, Father Leo Ward, a Holy Cross priest who would later help to shape Hesburgh's idea of a Catholic university, jotted down a warning: "If you don't learn to simplify your style with simple words, you will wind up being a pompous ass." Ted took the advice to heart, noting that his professor's own style was simple and direct.[20]

The summer after their first year as postulants (the first stage of joining a religious order), Hesburgh and his twenty-eight seminary classmates began a year-long novitiate (stage two) at Rolling Prairie, a dilapidated six-hundred-acre farm about thirty miles west of Notre Dame. The novitiate was intended as a break from the strictly academic curriculum of seminary formation—a time, right before taking vows, to pause and reflect on God's will for one's life. As Hesburgh later learned, the novitiate had another purpose: "to indoctrinate the incoming class of seminarians to the discipline and rigors of priesthood by exposing them to hard physical labor." It was, as Hesburgh put it, a kind of boot camp, "complete with rigorous physical training and a hard-nosed drill instructor."[21] The sergeant was Brother Seraphim, a former German soldier who immigrated to the United States after World War I, and who—in Hesburgh's estimation— seemed especially creative in finding ways to make hard work even harder.

The Holy Cross Fathers had purchased the farm just a few years before Hesburgh arrived, and it needed a lot of attention. With his classmates, Hesburgh cleared rocks, built a barn, painted a fifty-foot-tall silo (after moving it, cement block by cement block, from a nearby farm), felled trees and chopped wood for the furnace, cleared sumac brush, collected honey from angry bees, picked lice off sheep, shoveled manure, planted corn, harvested wheat, and washed thousands and thousands of dishes. The year left an impression on the young Hesburgh. In his autobiography, he dedicated ten pages to Rolling Prairie, including a two-page, stomach-turning account of butchering a pig. If one of the goals of the novitiate was to weed out those who didn't have the discipline to meet the demands of religious life, then the year seems to have been a success. The following summer, only nine of the original twenty-nine seminarians remained. Hesburgh was one of those still standing. For the most part, he found the manual labor a distraction from what he thought most important, their studies (despite the oppressive schedule, Hesburgh claimed to have read over a hundred books during his novitiate year). But he didn't complain or question. "I just knew I wanted to be a priest. I figured that if every priest I knew in the order went through that I guess I could go through it." He did come to an important realization, however. "I also learned I didn't want to be a farmer."[22]

In August of 1936, Hesburgh returned to Notre Dame to take his temporary vows of poverty, chastity, and obedience. He continued his studies, moving to the major seminary that stood on the banks of Saint Joseph's Lake. His priestly formation during this time—before, during, and after Rolling Prairie—could fairly be described as monastic. This may seem strange, considering that he was preparing to join an active religious order founded in the wake of the French Revolution for the purpose of preaching parish missions and educating the young. The Congregation of Holy Cross was established to serve the world, not to separate from it. However, Catholic theology at the start of the twentieth century emphasized the sacred identity of the priest as a man "set apart," standing as "another Christ" (*alter Christus*). Thus a monastic—almost cloistered—seminary experience seemed to be the logical way to shape such an identity. At Rolling Prairie, the seminarians worked like monks. They observed silence twenty-two hours a day, communicating at meals through hand signals. They sang the Divine Office at set times, just like in a monastery. They meditated, prayed, and listened to obscure religious texts read aloud while they ate. It was a structured spiritual life built around that ancient monastic motto, *ora et labora*, "pray and work."

Back at Notre Dame the same medieval rhythm continued. An article on life at the seminary several years later described a pattern that had been in place for generations. "There is Mass and Communion and meditation every morning; there is the recitation of the Little Office of the Blessed Virgin during the day, as well as spiritual reading and rosary; there are the countless reminders of his obligation such as the prayers before and after meals, the silence, the regimented schedule, and the bells which signal the end of one activity and the beginning of another."[23] Hesburgh grew to hate those bells commanding him to do this or do that, to go here or go there. "I never gave voice to those thoughts, you can be sure, because I had taken a vow of obedience, and mine was not to question my superiors."[24]

Hesburgh did not question his superiors' decision when, in July of 1937, on the cusp of starting his junior year at Notre Dame, Hesburgh was summoned (likely by a bell) to the office of Father Ted Mehling, the assistant superior. When Hesburgh walked into his office, Mehling looked up, handed him a piece of paper, and said, "This is for you. You're going to Rome to study next year."

Ted was stunned.

In the preface to his autobiography, Hesburgh reflected on the vows he had professed as a young man all those years ago. The most difficult of the three, he admitted, was neither poverty nor chastity, but obedience. "The vow of obedience is the hardest in that one gives up that most precious of divine gifts, freedom."[25] When Hesburgh and his classmate Tom McDonagh met with the provincial, Father James A. Burns, to ask why they were being sent to Rome, he told them that they were to earn doctorates in philosophy and theology. Burns acknowledged, "It will take some time, but you'll be able to do it because you're going to be there for eight years."

Eight years. Ted was excited about the prospect of going abroad. But the thought of being away from his family for so long gave him pause. It was hard to imagine. "When you're twenty years old, eight years is almost half your life."[26] But there was nothing to do. He had taken a vow of obedience. His path was set, and he accepted it. Despite the anxiety he felt at the time, in retrospect, Hesburgh saw the freedom that came with surrendering his freedom. "My whole life as a priest would have been vastly different, and probably less productive, had I been able to do what I wanted to do, instead of what I was assigned to do."[27] And so, eight weeks after meeting with Burns, Ted and his friend Tom boarded the *SS Champlain* and steamed across the sea to Rome.

CHAPTER TWO

Becoming a Theologian

For three years, Hesburgh lived and worked at the crossroads of a global church. "Rome was a new world—vast, different, somewhat frightening."[1] At the Jesuit-run Gregorian University, Hesburgh sat in classrooms filled with students from every country on earth. He got to know seminarians from Africa, who became his first black friends. A Mexican student chatted with him in Spanish between classes. The superior of the house where he lived, Father George Sauvage, was a tall Frenchman who expected everyone in the community to pray, read, and converse in French.

The daily routine in Rome was rigid: rise at five for prayer, followed by Mass, breakfast, classes, chapel, lunch, classes, an afternoon walk, chapel, supper, half-hour recreation, study, bed, and up again the next morning at five. The afternoon excursions were a welcome break from the regimen of study and prayer, and Hesburgh quickly came to enjoy his time exploring the Eternal City. The Holy Cross community occupied a three-story house on the Via dei Cappuccini, just a block away from the Piazza Barberini in the heart of Rome. Every day at three, rain or shine, all fourteen men living in the house—priests as well as seminarians—would line up and head out, two-by-two, in their long black cassocks and round, wide-brimmed hats. Hesburgh got to observe Roman life up close and took every opportunity he could to practice his Italian with the people he would pass in the street.

Hesburgh had always enjoyed learning languages, but in Rome he came to love them. Indeed, his immersion in languages was probably the most important thing Hesburgh took away from his time studying abroad. "I have no doubt that the fluency I acquired in Rome helped me enormously in all the work I was to do the rest of my life."[2] His lectures, textbooks, and oral exams at the university were all in Latin. He learned to speak French at home and Italian in the street. A friend taught him Spanish, and he taught himself German over an intense summer that he spent studying at a guest house in the Alps, near the Austrian border.

Hesburgh's discipline was impressive. He set a personal goal of learning ten new words in French, Italian, and German every day—claiming that, at the end of his first year in Rome, he had expanded his vocabulary by thirty-six hundred words in each language! "I made it a point never to speak English if I could avoid it."[3] His facility in learning new languages was the mark of a prodigious memory and an insatiable curiosity. However, for Hesburgh, it was always about making connections. Later in life Hesburgh explained his approach: "I just try to buy little phrase books to get me started in whatever language I'm about to encounter. Then I let the other person teach me what I don't know." Americans, he felt, were too self-conscious and just needed to plunge in. "Even little children can quickly pick up languages, so they're not all that hard. And by making the try you're making friends."[4]

In the 1930s, Gregorian University was a kind of Catholic West Point for future priests. Hesburgh was aware of the honor in being selected to study there. He knew that, back then, "those who went to the Gregorian most often ended up running things in one way or another."[5] Yet, in retrospect, Hesburgh admitted that his education at the "Greg" left a lot to be desired. Although he pursued a rigorous curriculum heavy in philosophy—with courses in logic, metaphysics, ethics, and epistemology—Hesburgh found the overall approach rigid and unimaginative. The "syllabus and instruction methods had not changed," Hesburgh opined, "from the way things were done when they started the university in 1558."[6]

Students may have come to Rome from many different countries, speaking many different languages, but they were all being taught to think in the same way. Hesburgh's seminary formation took place entirely within the era of neoscholasticism in theology. Neoscholasticism was a centuries-long attempt to revive the intellectual contributions of the great scholars (the "scholastics") of the Middle Ages—especially the contribution of the thirteenth-century Dominican Saint Thomas Aquinas. In 1879, Pope Leo XIII singled out the thought of Saint Thomas as *the* alternative to the many dangerous ideas circulating in the modern world. According to the pope, Thomism was the philosophy best able to offer a unified and coherent vision of reality, and he mandated that every seminary teach the thought of Saint Thomas as the foundation for theological studies.

In his own day, Aquinas was a creative genius, on the cutting edge of the new universities in Europe, bringing the Christian faith into dialogue with the recently recovered science of Aristotle, exploring the insights of Jewish and Islamic commentators, offering a synthetic view of the graced human person—and all of creation—flowing from and returning to God. In contrast to this open and constantly questioning approach, neoscholasticism was closed and defensive. For four hundred years, the Catholic Church had felt as if it were under attack. Enemies abounded—Protestant reformers, Enlightenment intellectuals, political revolutionaries, atheistic scientists—and they had to be defeated. Their worldview had to be rejected. In the seminary textbooks, or "manuals," that Hesburgh would have used, the open-ended "question" of Saint Thomas had become a definitive "thesis" proving that Catholics were right. "Each major subject was boiled down to fifteen propositions, and at the end of each course you had to defend any one of those fifteen theses that the examining professor picked at random, just as students before you had done for the past four hundred years."[7]

In a letter from the early 1970s, Hesburgh complained that this "controlled theology" had a "deadening influence" on his intellectual formation: "I was mainly asked to memorize during those seven years, and much that I memorized is no longer good theology after Vatican Council II."[8] However, if this would be Hesburgh's ultimate assessment of his Roman education, you wouldn't have known it at the time. Hesburgh threw himself into his philosophical and theological studies. He may have found the methods dull (learning Hebrew in Latin, Hesburgh joked, was not something he would recommend), but he mastered them. For years Hesburgh would echo neoscholastic assumptions about the relationship of faith and reason, the unity of knowledge, and the preeminence of Christian wisdom. He embraced the order, clarity, and confidence of the neoscholastic synthesis and seemed to take comfort in its promise of an integrated worldview centered on God. Even after he came to see its limitations, Hesburgh still acknowledged that his time at the Greg had two lasting effects. It instilled in him academic discipline, and it provided him a solid grounding in classical theology, which would serve as a secure intellectual home from which to explore new ideas.[9]

Hesburgh's capacity to explore new ideas and his energy for engaging the world around him must have come from somewhere other than his coursework. The impulse of seminary education at the time was to shut doors or throw up walls in order to keep the world out. During his first two years in Rome, the Holy Cross house had no newspapers and no radio. Thus Hesburgh had a fairly limited sense of what was going on. "Vaguely we realized that war in Europe was being talked about," he recalled, but it did not seem to loom large in his consciousness.

Hesburgh had arrived in Europe in the fall of 1937. In May of the following year, after Germany annexed Austria, Hitler made a state visit to Rome. In true propaganda style, Mussolini rolled out the red carpet. He renamed a street after the German leader, organized tours of historical sites and military parades, and cloaked the city in swastikas. Since Mussolini's official quarters were right behind the Gregorian in the Quirinale, classes were canceled for a week so that the rooftop could be secured. On one occasion, Hitler's entourage passed along the Via Sistina, only a hundred or so feet from the Holy Cross residence, with *der Führer* taking in the sights from an open car. When a classmate, Bill Shriner, saw him from the window, he called out, "Come over here and look out. Hitler is passing." Hesburgh later boasted that he didn't budge. "I wouldn't walk ten feet to see that bum,"[10] was his reply.

Events in Europe, however, were already in motion. When the Nazis invaded Poland on September 1, 1939, the Holy Cross community learned about it on the radio Father Sauvage had finally purchased for the house. In May of 1940, the

American consul in Rome interrupted morning classes at the Greg to announce that the Nazis had invaded the Low Countries. All Americans were to leave Rome immediately. They would be evacuated on the *USS Manhattan*, which was leaving from Genoa in a few days. "The announcement that we were going home threw us all into a frenzy."[11] With the term cut short by a month, Hesburgh and his classmates had one week to complete their final exams, pack up, and get ready to leave. Following a nine-day voyage, Hesburgh arrived in New York on June 10, the same day that Italy invaded southern France. Paris would fall within the week. Hesburgh had escaped the war, but the war and its effects would shape Hesburgh's life for years to come.

What was supposed to have been an eight-year course of study had been cut to three. Hesburgh left Rome with a bachelor of philosophy degree, not the doctorate his provincial had expected. (Years later, the Notre Dame board realized that, because Hesburgh's undergraduate degree was from the Greg, their famous president had never graduated from Notre Dame—an unacceptable gap in his resume remedied by the conferral of an honorary degree in 1984.) Hesburgh would pick up his seminary training in the fall at Holy Cross College in Washington, right next door to Catholic University of America. Three years later, on June 24, 1943, in the sanctuary of Sacred Heart Church on the campus of Notre Dame, Hesburgh received what he called the greatest grace of his life: he became a priest.

At the first Mass of a newly ordained Holy Cross priest a few years later, Hesburgh homilized: "No one but a fellow priest will really know what it meant to kneel before the Bishop in Sacred Heart Church . . . to feel the hands of that successor of the Apostles on his head, to have his own hands anointed with consecrated oil, to touch the chalice and host of Sacrifice, to be clad with the sacred Vestments of the Mass, to hear the words that engraved upon his soul the eternal and indelible mark of Christ the Priest." To be a priest was the central fact of Hesburgh's life, the word he wanted written on his tombstone, the highest calling he could imagine, the one and only thing he had ever hoped to be. To the family and friends of that newly ordained priest, Hesburgh preached: "You could search far and wide in this world without finding a Vision quite so noble or quite so ennobling as that of Christ's Priesthood. And the reason is that this Vision is the Very Vision of Christ Himself. The Priest is a priest because he is consecrated and committed to be what Christ *is*, to do what Christ *did*. The Priest, more than anything else, is another Christ."[12]

Hesburgh's rather exalted vision of the priesthood was neither original nor unusual. It reflected the common assumption among Catholics at the time that the priest was a special and holy person, a man set apart for the things of God, empowered to act "in the person of Christ" (*in persona Christi*) and to stand as "another Christ" (*alter Christus*) before humanity. This vision was crafted in the seventeenth century by French spiritual writers; it was handed down in the nineteenth century by religious orders such as Holy Cross; and it was sustained in the early twentieth century by the thick religious culture of immigrant Catholics in communities across the United States.

Within this widely shared understanding of priesthood, the element that most captured Hesburgh's imagination—from the very beginning of his ministry to the very end—was the idea that the priest served as a *mediator* between God and humanity. In the work of mediation the priest shares in the mission of the great High Priest, Jesus Christ. Sin had opened up a wide chasm between God and the human race.

Into that void stepped Jesus. "Christ was the perfect go-between, since He was both Perfect God and Perfect Man." The divine Son lived and worked among people, "bringing them closer to God and bringing God closer to them."[13] Hesburgh saw his own priesthood as a graced participation in the very same priesthood of Christ. However, in Hesburgh's estimation, such an exalted role did not set the priest apart from other people—elevated over humanity and removed from the concerns of the world. The priest had to be close both to God *and* to God's people. He was called to be "a Christlike go-between," bridging the gap between heaven and earth through his counsel and guidance, his witness and preaching, his absolution in the confessional, and, in a special way, his offering of the Mass.

Of all the duties of the priest, the most important to Hesburgh, without question, was to offer the sacrifice of the Mass. To celebrate Mass as a priest was to exercise a spiritual power beyond compare—the power "to speak in the name of Christ and to renew the priestly Mystery [of] Christ's eternal sacrifice on Calvary, to bring God again into our midst as our Saviour and Lord." No wonder, the young Hesburgh preached, that we bow our heads at the moment of consecration, "for here is a power that not even the Blessed Virgin Mary nor the Angels have."[14] At his ordination, Hesburgh made a personal pledge to celebrate Mass every day of his life. Back home in Syracuse, Hesburgh would proudly walk to Most Holy Rosary Church for morning Mass carrying his newly crafted golden chalice, a gift from family and friends. Later on, as a globe-trotting university president, Hesburgh always carried with him a more modest Mass kit, equipped with a tiny altar cloth, chalice, cruets for wine and water, crucifix, and candles. Hesburgh's autobiography shares stories of offering Mass all around the world, from a Russian Orthodox chapel in Moscow to an icebreaker sixty miles off the coast of Antarctica. Hesburgh celebrated Mass in grand European ballrooms and seedy airport hotels, aboard lurching trains and nuclear submarines, in African villages and Mexican huts. Hesburgh even figured out a way to set up a portable altar inside the space shuttle, were he ever to realize his dream of being the first priest to say Mass in space.

Hesburgh's commitment to the Eucharist was fierce. Asked if he had to choose between being president of the United States and offering Mass, the answer would be easy: he would offer Mass. "If the only way I had to celebrate the Eucharist tomorrow morning was to walk 20 miles," he once told an interviewer, "I would start walking tonight."[15] "He'd say Mass if he had pneumonia, or stomach flu, or the bubonic plague," said Edmund Stephan, Hesburgh's long-time friend and former chair of the Notre Dame board.[16]

The only time Hesburgh remembered ever missing daily Mass was the night he helped keep vigil over a premature baby. After baptizing the three-pound, eight-ounce newborn, Hesburgh passed a water fountain in the hospital hallway and, without thinking, took a drink. He realized a moment later that it was past midnight. He had broken his eucharistic fast and thus, according to the rules at the time, he was not allowed to offer Mass that day. If Hesburgh ever regretted that sip of water, he never regretted that night. The baby, Mark O'Connor, survived and would go on to graduate from Notre Dame.

Hesburgh was ordained during the war and his dream was to serve as a Navy chaplain on an aircraft carrier in the Pacific. However, his provincial superior wanted Hesburgh back in Washington to finish his studies. "Get your doctorate now, or you will never get it," Father Thomas Steiner told him. "Then we'll talk about your becoming a Navy chaplain."[17] It had to be clear to Hesburgh then and there that his community had other plans for him.

When he returned to DC in the summer of 1943, Hesburgh threw himself into his priestly ministry, while at the same time determined to finish a three-year doctorate in two. He was soon directing a retreat for high school students, ministering to troubled kids at the National Training School for Boys, attending seminars on racial justice, and assisting at various parishes in the area. He met great priests who proved to be excellent mentors. His first pastor, Father Bill at Saint Martin's parish, was warm and cheerful, full of enormous energy and goodwill. He encouraged Hesburgh never to worry about being cheated by those coming to the door asking for a handout: "Better to be conned ninety-nine times than to miss the one who really needs help."[18] Another priest, Father George Di Prizio at Saint Patrick's, cautioned: "Ted, don't be too professional." By that he meant that a priest should never treat people as if they were items on a to-do list or widgets on an assembly line. "'A good priest will spend time with the person at the door. He won't be satisfied until he knows why that person rang the bell.' *Priesthood means service, no matter who rings the bell.*"[19]

What seemed to most energize Hesburgh was ministering to the many servicemen and servicewomen who passed through the nation's capital in those years. Through Father Tom Dade, who hosted a popular radio program, Hesburgh got involved in the Washington USO club. Located in the Knights of Columbus Hall at Tenth and K Streets, the club's goal was to provide a wholesome alternative to the other diversions of the red-light district. To do that, the club sponsored huge dances, bringing in some of the best military bands in the country, often with two or three bands playing at the same time on different floors. Hesburgh would circulate throughout the night, keeping an eye on "a thousand or fifteen hundred jitterbugging men and women" in uniform having a great time.[20]

In addition to volunteering at the club, Hesburgh partnered up with another Holy Cross priest, Father Charlie Sheedy, to put out a series of religious pamphlets for those serving in the military. One pocket-sized booklet, *For God and County*, ran to three million copies, Hesburgh estimated. Another booklet, which Hesburgh wrote himself, was intended for young women in the service. Titled *Letters to Servicewomen*, the text consisted of simple advice for coping with life in the military. Modeled on letters that Hesburgh might have written to his own sisters, each chapter began, "Dear Mary, Bets, and Anne." What followed were words you would expect to hear from a priest who also happened to be your brother: Try to do little things, like typing a letter or answering the phone, for the glory of God. Try to take an interest in the other women around you. Practice the "virtue of consideration." Be charitable. Be patient. Above all, be kind. "[Y]ou will find that since kindness and a practical interest in people are the most irresistible powers for good, you can't help but do good if you are kind."[21]

At the same time, be careful. Life in the service offered opportunities for exercising the Christian virtues, but it also presented dangers. A woman's body "is the Temple of God," and some men cannot be trusted with it. "Keep them at arm's length. Don't go out with them. Never be alone with them." Be especially careful with alcohol, it will "sell you short every time. Some ways of talking and walking and carrying on generally cheapen you."[22]

In these little letters, we catch a glimpse of Hesburgh's early views on sexuality and gender. At a time when the demands of war were upsetting traditional gender roles, Hesburgh was thoroughly conventional. Women "very definitely have their own place in the world, but it is not man's place." Instead, their place is in the home and in the family. Their elevated vocation is to serve as "the inspirer of man." Whenever "women have stepped off their pedestal and sought false freedom and liberty, they have ended in the lowest kind of slavery—without love, without true friends, with nothing but bitter emptiness to their lives."[23]

Hesburgh later admitted that, in retrospect, the advice he doled out in *Letters to Servicewomen* sounds rather quaint. But he insisted that he ran his drafts by the women he knew at the USO, taking their concerns and suggestions into account. If today we judge Hesburgh's early views as paternalistic or sexist, we shouldn't be surprised to find such sentiments coming from a young priest in the 1940s trying to offer moral counsel to women.

Throughout his formation and into the first decades of his professional life, Hesburgh's world was almost exclusively male. Seminary classrooms and common rooms, community meals, faculty lounges, administrative offices, university meetings, boardrooms, commissions and committees—these were all male spaces dominated by men. However, this one-sided world, and his own celibate lifestyle, did not make Hesburgh uncomfortable or awkward with women. Hesburgh enjoyed close relationships with all of his sisters, especially Mary. His understanding of women's experience grew through his ministry in the confessional, his experience counseling women and married couples, and the many friendships he formed over the years.

More than anything, it was his vocation as a priest that drew Hesburgh into the lives of women. He found celibacy an incredibly liberating experience, one that freed him to relate to women in ways that he could not had he been married. Exceptionally charming and "movie-star handsome," Hesburgh attracted the wives of faculty members and government officials into his orbit at social events—a dynamic that Hesburgh attributed to the fact that, as a priest, he was "out of circulation" and thus "safe" for intimate conversation. While Hesburgh acknowledged the challenges that celibacy posed and the self-discipline it required ("we were not promised a rose garden"), his life gave witness to a healthy, integrated sexuality. As his biographer Michael O'Brien put it, "Perhaps even Fr. Theodore Hesburgh occasionally had a roving eye or entertained an errant desire, but there was never a hint of sexual indiscretion in his long, celibate career."[24]

After the Second Vatican Council, as Hesburgh watched thousands of men leave the priesthood, and as he came to appreciate the challenges faced by priests serving in remote areas, Hesburgh grew more open to the idea of allowing priests to marry. However, it was never something that he seriously considered for himself. He found his life as a priest too rewarding. He treasured too much the total availability for service made possible by celibacy. Asked late in life if he would do it all over again, if he were to return to his eighteen-year-old self, would he again vow celibacy for the rest of his life? Hesburgh answered yes, "but only on the same premise that led me to do it the first time: that vowing celibacy would make me a better priest."[25]

During his time in Washington, Hesburgh worked at a feverish pace. Not only was he volunteering with the USO, writing pamphlets, and helping out in parishes, he was also taking classes and cranking out page after page of his dissertation. Hesburgh had landed on a novel topic for his thesis, "the theology of the laity." His advisor at Catholic

University, Father Gene Burke, warned him: "It's a great idea, but you'll never get it approved at this university, because the subject is much too practical."[26]

At the time Hesburgh was writing his dissertation, Catholic theologians in Europe were just beginning to turn their attention to the "apostolate of the laity." The idea was that the laity should be active in the mission of the church, just like the apostles, helping to extend the church's influence into the secular world. Several lay associations—often grouped under the term "Catholic Action"—formed to support such apostolic works. Popes Pius XI and Pius XII saw these movements as a valuable response to secularization and so promoted Catholic Action aggressively. Their assumption was that the laity would follow the lead of the clergy: they were to be the "long arms" of the hierarchy, extending the clergy's influence into the world of work, politics, and culture. When Pius XI defined Catholic Action as "the participation of the laity in the apostolate of the hierarchy," he underscored this hierarchical assumption: laity share in work that really belongs to the ordained.

However, Hesburgh was inspired by other currents that had begun to surface in Europe. Rather than waiting for a mandate from the hierarchy before joining in the apostolate, Hesburgh believed that the laity received their mandate directly from Christ in baptism and confirmation. The laity are always to work under the guidance of the clergy, Hesburgh acknowledged, but their mission flows from their own fundamental identity as baptized and confirmed Christians—an identity that sacramental theology described as an "indelible character" imprinted on the soul. Indeed, Hesburgh's dissertation, which he published as *The Theology of Catholic Action*, was originally titled "The Relation of the Sacramental Characters of Baptism and Confirmation to the Lay Apostolate."

What is fascinating about Hesburgh's interest in the laity is how closely it fit into how he understood his own identity as a priest. The work of a priest is fundamentally one of mediation, of drawing together sinful humanity and the holy God. The work of the laity is, in its own way, also one of mediation. Hesburgh began his dissertation with the countercultural triumphalism characteristic of 1940s American Catholicism. He pointed to a godless secularism as the root of all evils plaguing the modern world. Secularism had driven a wedge between the temporal and the spiritual realms, cutting human society off from God. Hesburgh argued that the best hope for overcoming this split was the Christian layperson. Having a foot in both the world and the church, the layperson was "a perfect bridge" between the two.[27] Hesburgh's image of the priest as mediator was not new. What was new was the way in which Catholic theologians in Europe had begun to extend this notion of mediation to include the laity, who exercise their own priesthood, the priesthood of all the faithful. Due to his facility in languages, his active intellect, and his attraction to the practical, Hesburgh was able to pick up on a conversation that most American Catholics had not noticed. It was the conversation that would lead to Vatican II's unambiguous affirmation of the lay apostolate.

As planned, Hesburgh wrapped up his doctoral studies a year ahead of schedule and again wrote to his provincial to ask about becoming a Navy chaplain. "I would still like very much to do a priest's work with the boys who still have a man-sized job on their hands in the Pacific," he told Father Thomas Steiner in May 1945. Hesburgh argued that the chaplaincy would give him experience working with young people and prepare him for ministering to veterans after the war. "While taking the liberty to state my side," Hesburgh concluded his letter, "I am glad that the decision is entirely in your hands and will do to the best of my ability, whatever you decide."[28]

Steiner decided that Notre Dame needed a theologian more than the Navy needed a chaplain, so he assigned Hesburgh to teach at the university.[29] To soften the blow, Steiner explained that the Navy was sending thousands of candidates to Notre Dame for officer training, and the school was desperate for faculty. Hesburgh returned to campus in July of 1945. Two months later, the war in the Pacific ended, and the veterans' era in higher education began.

The G.I. Bill brought thousands of new students to Notre Dame. Highly motivated vets filled classrooms to take required courses in philosophy and theology. Worldly-wise and independent young men crammed into residence halls governed by outdated rules. Married students—a new phenomenon at Notre Dame—packed into surplus army barracks set up on the edge of campus.

Seeing his dream of becoming a Navy chaplain in a new light, Hesburgh threw himself into ministry among these new students. He helped establish the Notre Dame Veterans Club and became its first chaplain. Within a year, the veteran population swelled to nearly three-quarters of the student population, making the club superfluous. So Hesburgh turned his attention to married veterans, a group that would become very special to the young priest.

From 1945 to 1948, Hesburgh served as chaplain of "Vetville," a temporary neighborhood that provided married student housing in the form of thirty-nine repurposed prisoner-of-war barracks shipped to campus from a military camp in Missouri. At the height of the post-war surge, 117 families called Vetville their home. It was a tightly knit group of families, Hesburgh recalled, all facing the same kinds of problems. "They were newly married. They had babies. They were trying to make ends meet on a tight budget. Dad was in school. Mom was at home. When tragedy struck, you could really see how deeply they cared about each other."[30] Hesburgh was a part of it all. He baptized infants, heard confessions, and celebrated Mass. He counseled couples in the middle of the night, organized dances for the weekends, and even went door-to-door collecting coins to help a grieving couple bury their newborn. Despite the challenges, Hesburgh always looked back on his time at Vetville as one of the graces of his priestly life.

In many ways Hesburgh's ministry among the married students went hand-in-glove with his primary responsibility, teaching. When he arrived as a new faculty member, Hesburgh discovered that the Religion Department was one of the weakest at Notre Dame, with the "worst-taught courses" offering students "a painful choice" of options, with one course "as boring or as confusing as another."[31] Hesburgh was first assigned to cover moral theology. He later taught dogmatic theology and a new course he created on the theology of marriage. Frustrated with the dry and pedantic textbooks he was handed, Hesburgh wrote his own. Published in 1950 as part of a series of textbooks written by Holy Cross priests, *God and the World of Man* introduced Catholic doctrine concerning God, creation, the fall, and the redemption of humanity. The text is demanding in its attention to neoscholastic definitions and distinctions, revealing Hesburgh's commitment to theology as first and foremost an *intellectual* enterprise. The Catholic faith, he believed, offered a comprehensive and coherent worldview, able to withstand rigorous inquiry. There was no need to water down its truth—but that didn't mean the truth had to be inaccessible or uninspiring. *God and the World of Man* presents the Catholic doctrinal worldview in a style that is clear and easy to read, marked by references to recent *Time* magazine articles, battlefield vignettes, vivid illustrations, and glimpses of humor. Clearly Hesburgh had in mind the young men who were his students—former G.I.s and rising professionals. He appealed to their faith and their idealism, trying to show them "the wisdom that really matters, that teaches to live rather than merely to make a living."[32]

It was this wisdom, brought out most clearly in the church's theological tradition, that would serve as a kind of touchstone for Hesburgh as he moved, within a few short years, into his new role as president of the University of Notre Dame.

CHAPTER THREE

The Pursuit of Excellence

In his autobiography, Hesburgh described the day he became the fifteenth president of the University of Notre Dame. His predecessor, Father John Cavanaugh, was finishing up a six-year term, and the Holy Cross community had gathered for their annual retreat. As the provincial handed out "obediences"—the various assignments for the coming year—he announced to the room: "Ted Hesburgh, president." Everyone knew it was coming, but still Hesburgh's stomach flipped. "I was shaken with an attack of nerves."

As he walked out of the chapel, still absorbing the weight of the responsibility, Hesburgh fell into step with Cavanaugh. The outgoing president reached into the pocket of his cassock, pulled out the key to his office, and handed it to Hesburgh. "By the way," Cavanaugh said, "I promised to give a talk tonight to the Christian Family Movement over at Veterans Hall. Now that you're the president, you have to do it. Good luck. I'm off to New York."[1]

"Just like that," Hesburgh recalled, "I was president of the University of Notre Dame." No faculty committees, no search firms, no contract negotiations. No presidential inauguration, no speeches. "Just go right to work. That's the way it was done in 1952."[2]

Hesburgh was just thirty-five years old when he took office. He would serve the next thirty-five years as president. To say that Hesburgh was a transformational leader hardly does justice to the impact he had on the institution. Under his leadership, Notre Dame's annual operating budget went from $9.7 million in 1952 to $176.6 million in 1987. The endowment grew from $9 million to $350 million, and research funding from $735,000 to $15 million. Enrollment increased from 4,979 to 9,600, and the number of faculty rose from 389 to 950.[3] Moreover, in the midst of all this growth, Hesburgh guided Notre Dame through two historic transitions: the transfer of the university from the Congregation of the Holy Cross to a predominantly lay board of trustees in 1967, and the admission of women to the undergraduate program in 1972. All of this he accomplished (with a lot of help from others, Hesburgh would be quick to add) while maintaining a crushing schedule of off-campus commitments. "Just go right to work" was exactly what Hesburgh did.

Early in his presidency, Hesburgh articulated for himself a singular goal: "I envisioned Notre Dame as a great *Catholic* university, the greatest in the world!"[4] There were many great universities, but not since the Middle Ages, Hesburgh believed, had there been a great *Catholic* university. For Notre Dame to become great, it needed great students, great faculty, and great facilities. All of that required a great deal of money! It also required great vision.

Hesburgh began to flesh out that vision in his first presidential address to faculty in the fall of 1952. He spoke about Christian wisdom—about the world's need for wisdom and the university's mission to inculcate it. Wisdom concerns an understanding of the whole; and *Christian* wisdom understands the whole of creation in relationship to God, who is both source and destiny of all things. This Christian wisdom "unites all that is true." It provides an ordered view of the world, offers a hierarchical division of the disciplines, and gives a pattern of ordered education for the student.[5] In other speeches from the early 1950s, Hesburgh explained that the key to cultivating this wisdom at the university was the presence of theology as an academic discipline. Here he drew liberally from John Henry Newman's classic nineteenth-century text *The Idea of a University*, which was enjoying a resurgence of interest among American educators at the time. Newman had argued that theology was necessary in the university because a university, by its very nature, professes to teach all knowledge. Were it not to teach the knowledge of God—theology—it would not be teaching *all* knowledge, and thus it would not be a university in the full and true sense. Moreover, because all knowledge—human and divine—is ultimately one, theology is essential for "completing, integrating and correcting" all other disciplines.[6]

In his early years as president, Hesburgh accepted a common Catholic narrative: powerful currents unleashed by the Reformation and the Enlightenment made "the ordered flow of knowledge a swirling, churning vortex of conflicting assertions and denials." Amidst this disarray, only the Catholic university could bring order to the human quest for understanding. "Here is an apostolate that no secular university today can undertake—for they are largely cut off from the tradition of adequate knowledge which comes only through faith in the mind and faith in God, the highest wisdom of Christian philosophy and Catholic theology."[7] Because of its commitment to theology, Hesburgh believed, the Catholic university was uniquely positioned to meet the challenge of the times.

Hesburgh's vision, though articulated with unusual clarity and conviction, was hardly controversial at a place like Notre Dame. A few months after his inauguration, Hesburgh launched a massive self-study of the liberal arts curriculum. The final report, written by the philosophy professor Vincent E. Smith, began with the bald claim that theology (along with philosophy in its "subsidiary" role) was the linchpin to curricular integration at the university. The three-hundred-page report that followed never questioned this basic premise. Indeed, one of the methods the review team used to gather data for the report was a series of interdepartmental colloquia in which faculty from all of the other departments with required courses were expected to discuss how theology and philosophy related to their work![8] A revised curriculum based on the report was implemented in the fall of 1953.

The confidence that Catholicism had the intellectual resources to confront modern skepticism, secularism, and confusion did not mean that Catholic universities had risen to the challenge. Hesburgh was blunt: "But it is nothing short of wishful thinking or vincible ignorance to claim that we are anywhere near accomplishing the true function of theology in most of our own universities."[9]

The problems at Notre Dame, however, extended far beyond the theology department. Before becoming president, Hesburgh served for three years as Executive Vice President under his dynamic mentor John Cavanaugh. Cavanaugh, quick to notice Hesburgh's abilities, put him in charge of implementing a major administrative reorganization. Hesburgh wrote up procedures, job descriptions, and lines of authority for five newly constituted vice presidents. He was charged with reorganizing the powerful athletics department and put in charge of all construction projects on campus, including five new buildings (Nieuwland, O'Shaughnessy, and Fisher Halls, the Morris Inn, and the power plant) and several significant renovations. This on-the-job training "was swift and awesome."[10] It also gave Hesburgh a clear-eyed view of Notre Dame's challenges. In an early memo to Cavanaugh, Hesburgh offered a litany of financial woes facing the university, concluding, "Maybe we should begin the budget meetings with a prayer to the Holy Spirit and end them with a Hail Mary."[11] In another letter sent to Cavanaugh on August 3, 1951, Hesburgh provided his frank assessment of the problems facing the university, most of which had to do with poor administrative leadership.

When Hesburgh became president, he moved quickly to replace those he saw as ineffective leaders. With Cavanaugh's help, he removed the dean of the Law School, replacing him with a successful Columbus attorney, Joseph O'Meara, who expelled half of the law students (anyone who had failed one or more courses), tightened entrance requirements, revised the curriculum, and set new standards for faculty. Hesburgh dismissed the director of Notre Dame's scientific research lab, the head of the history institute, the Business College dean, and the dean of the College of Arts and Letters, Father Frank Cavanaugh, who happened to be the former president's brother. With John's blessing, Hesburgh replaced Frank with his friend and publishing partner Father Charlie Sheedy, who would serve as dean for nineteen years.

In his autobiography, Hesburgh was curt in his assessment of the various administrators he inherited: "He refused to change, and he had to go. . . . When the director . . . resisted our changes, he had to go. . . . That was the end of him as dean. . . ." Hesburgh acknowledged that firing people was, "without doubt, the worst part of administration." In retrospect, he admitted, he could have handled some of these situations with more finesse, "but I did what needed to be done as best I could at the time."[12]

What drove Hesburgh's decision-making was the relentless pursuit of academic excellence. When Hesburgh took office in 1952, Notre Dame was well known for excellence—but it was on the football field, not in the classroom. A legend in his own time, Notre Dame's coach, Frank Leahy, had led his "lads" to four national championships, five undefeated seasons (a sixth would come in 1953), and a thirty-nine-game unbeaten streak. But Hesburgh bristled at the characterization of Notre Dame as a "football factory." He was irked when he showed up at press conferences attended only by sportswriters. At one event organized on the West Coast early in his presidency, a reporter asked him to pose with a football in the hiking position. Hesburgh refused and privately vowed to banish Notre Dame's image as a football school.[13]

Such sacrilege might have condemned a lesser man. Hesburgh was astute enough to recognize that football had put the "Fighting Irish" on the map, and that it provided the financial resources needed to transform Notre Dame into a great Catholic university. He wanted the Irish to win, but he also wanted athletics to take their proper place in an institution whose academic mission was primary.

No doubt Hesburgh's attitude toward football was colored by his earlier confrontations with Leahy before becoming president. One of the first things Father Cavanaugh asked Hesburgh to do after appointing him executive vice president was to reorganize the athletics department. The size and success of the football program meant that Leahy—who was both head coach and athletic director—did whatever he wanted, operating largely independent of university administration. Cavanaugh wanted more oversight and accountability, and he asked Hesburgh to make it happen. The assignment filled Hesburgh, who had just turned thirty-two, with dread: "So, essentially, my job was to 'reorganize' the domain of Notre Dame's football coach, who happened to be the most famous, most talented football coach in the country—the great Frank Leahy. . . . He was a man no one, least of all a very green executive vice president, could expect to push around."[14]

Hesburgh spent the summer of 1949 reviewing procedures and issuing new directives. He reigned in the loose practice of handing out complimentary tickets to games. He gave the team doctor absolute authority in determining whether an injured athlete could play. He cut the traveling squad for football to thirty-eight, bringing Notre Dame in line with Big Ten Conference rules. And he persuaded the head basketball coach, Ed "Moose" Krause, to step down and take over the role of athletic director, a newly configured position that supervised the football coach and reported to the executive vice president.

Hesburgh knew Leahy would be furious, and he warned Cavanaugh that the changes would not go over well. He would have to decide whom he was going to support— Leahy or Hesburgh. Cavanaugh assured Hesburgh that he had his full support. "You might very well lose your football coach in the process," Hesburgh pointed out. Cavanaugh replied, "Well, we can survive that."[15]

Despite a tense showdown that fall over the size of the travel team—where Leahy ultimately backed down—Notre Dame survived the reorganization without losing either a football coach or an executive vice president. Hesburgh and Leahy made peace and went on to work together for another four years. After becoming president, Hesburgh helped encourage the intense Leahy to retire early—despite finishing the 1953 season undefeated—in order to care for his deteriorating health. His replacement was the twenty-five-year-old alum and freshman coach Terry Brennan. After a successful start, Brennan's teams faltered, and Hesburgh felt compelled to let him go at the end of his five-year contract.

Firing the young, popular coach just a few days before Christmas in 1958 unleashed a torrent of criticism. "I came off like Scrooge," Hesburgh later complained.[16] *Sports Illustrated* accused Hesburgh of "surrender."[17] By firing Brennan, the article implied, Hesburgh had given in to alumni who only cared about football and had thus given up on his dream of academic excellence.

Two weeks later, *SI* published Hesburgh's defiant response. *Excellence* is always the goal, he argued, excellence in everything the university does. "Most of my waking hours are directed to the achievement of that excellence here in the academic order. As long as we, like most American universities, are engaged in intercollegiate athletics, we will strive for excellence of performance in this area too, but never at the expense of the primary order of academic excellence." Hesburgh accused critics of a skewed perspective. A university can appoint twenty distinguished professors in its promotion of excellence and hardly attract a ripple of attention. But when that same university makes "a well-considered change in athletic personnel for the same reason," it is accused of caving. "There has indeed been a surrender at Notre Dame," Hesburgh concluded, "but it is a surrender to excellence on all fronts, and in this we hope to rise above ourselves with the help of God."[18]

Hesburgh's drive for excellence "on all fronts" meant that Notre Dame was soon a university racing to keep up with its president. Charlie Sheedy remembers watching Hesburgh sprint through the early years of his presidency "as though shot from a cannon." The man had enormous energy.

"Moxie," Sheedy said of Hesburgh, "boy, he had the moxie."[19]

During Hesburgh's first six-year term, twelve new buildings sprang up on campus; the first comprehensive faculty manual was approved; new curricula were implemented in the undergraduate program, in the law school, and in the business school; admission standards tightened; more than a hundred PhDs were added to the faculty; salaries increased by half; and the endowment more than doubled.

A 1956 *Time* magazine article described Hesburgh as a "hustler for quality," hammering away at alumni across the country about the importance of raising the academic profile of their alma mater. When one older alum asked, "What about the ordinary boy? Why can't he find a place at Notre Dame?" Hesburgh replied, "What do you drive, a jalopy or a Cadillac?" The alum smiled, "a Cadillac." Clearly, Hesburgh would not rest until Notre Dame became known as a university of Cadillac quality. Commenting on the decision to cap enrollment to improve standards, Hesburgh said, "We decided that it was more important to turn out one well-educated, competent man than 100 mediocrities." After documenting the impressive strides made at Notre Dame in such a short time, Hesburgh concluded that, still, "We've got a long way to go."[20]

Historically, the president of Notre Dame served as religious superior of the Holy Cross community on campus—an ecclesiastical office limited by canon law to a maximum of six years. At the end of Hesburgh's term in 1958, the community decided he was far too important to the university to step down, so they separated out the role of superior, and reappointed Hesburgh president. "I took those first six years like a 100-yard dash," he later said. "Then when I got to the tape, I had to keep going."[21]

By 1958, Hesburgh had developed a regular, though un-usual, work rhythm. When he wasn't traveling, Hesburgh's days started late, with prayer, Mass, and a light breakfast, and ramped up from there. In the office by noon, he handled meetings, calls, visitors, and mail for the rest of the day. At 5:30 p.m. he joined his community for prayers and dinner. After dinner, he went back to his office and put in another eight hours at his desk. He regularly worked past 3 a.m. ("I just get warmed up at that time of night"), appreciating the quiet and the freedom from interruptions. Hesburgh juggled multiple problems simultaneously, guided by a few axioms: "never handle the same piece of paper twice; never have two people worrying about the same thing."[22]

Hesburgh's management style was to pick the best people and delegate—and he had an incredible eye for talent. His closest collaborator, bar none, was a Holy Cross priest his own age, Father Ned Joyce, whom Hesburgh appointed to his old job, executive vice president, as soon as he took of-fice. Joyce was a certified public accountant who, in his thirty-five years as executive vice president, "reigned over finances, buildings and grounds, university relations, athlet-ics, and everything else"—everything, Hesburgh gracefully and gratefully admitted, that he himself was not good at.[23] Although they differed in skill-set, temperament, and po-litical persuasion, and although they often disagreed—or maybe because of their differences—the two made a perfect pair, complementing each other well all the way to retire-ment and beyond.

Next to Joyce, the most important person to Hesburgh at Notre Dame was Helen Hosinski, who served as his admin-istrative assistant for all thirty-five years in the president's office. Hesburgh joked that the office never needed a com-puter, so sharp was Hosinski's memory and so efficient her organization. "She ran the office and she ran much of my life with nary a misstep or mistake, an extraordinary woman."[24]

Hesburgh knew he needed help, but he also knew he had to make the important decisions. Due to the slowness of deliberation and the diversity of viewpoints endemic to university life, Hesburgh felt he had to take charge. In meetings with faculty, administrators, board members, or students, Hesburgh always dominated. Once his opinion on a matter was made known, the outcome was inevitable. He trusted his instincts and brought a moral compass to every decision. The most important advice he said he ever got from his mentor John Cavanaugh was simple: "You don't make a decision because it's going to be popular, or because it's going to be cheap or expedient. You make a decision because you think it is right."[25]

Hesburgh's consistency, fair-mindedness, and strength of character earned him the respect and appreciation of the faculty. According to legendary English professor Frank O'Malley, despite the incredible success of those early years, with the many tangible signs of improvement, Hesburgh's greatest accomplishment at Notre Dame was the atmosphere he created. "It is an atmosphere of freedom and flexibility and good will, an atmosphere that has made of this university a human as well as an academic community." Said another faculty member, "He always gave us the impression we were doing something terrific here."[26]

This was a time of widespread obsession with "excellence" in American higher education—a period of angst captured best by the influential 1958 report of the Rockefeller Fund, *The Pursuit of Excellence: Education and the Future of America*. Published less than a year after the launch of Sputnik, *The Pursuit of Excellence* detailed the weaknesses of the American educational system and proposed a series of institutional changes. The psychological trauma of falling behind in the space race—and, by implication, falling behind in math, science, and education in general—spurred soul-searching among Catholic and non-Catholic educators alike. Catholics, however, felt a particular insecurity, given a history of keeping their distance from "modern" developments in science and scholarship. An explosive 1955 article by the prominent Catholic historian John Tracy Ellis drew attention to the dearth of Catholic scholars in every field, unleashing a torrent of pent-up Catholic self-criticism. "Where are the Catholic Salks, Oppenheimers, Einsteins?" asked Hesburgh's predecessor, John Cavanaugh, in a 1957 speech that was quoted for years.[27]

Hesburgh, who served on the Rockefeller task force that wrote *The Pursuit of Excellence*, was unsparing in his criticism of Catholic complacency. In a 1961 address to the National Catholic Education Association, he called out Catholic parochialism and the failures of its educational institutions to confront the pressing challenges of the modern world—from scientific advances to race relations. His remarks caused an uproar at the convention, with observers appealing for a moratorium on this Catholic self-flagellation. "But, let us admit it frankly," Hesburgh argued, "much failure has been our own fault: of persons and institutions, often enough through laziness, lack of vision or the mercenary spirit, sometimes through abysmal mediocrity and just plain bad teaching and bad learning."[28] The following year, *Time* featured Hesburgh on the cover, asking the question, "Where are the Catholic intellectuals?" Inside, the magazine profiled Notre Dame and its charismatic president. It highlighted the spectacular growth of the institution but also noted a persistent inferiority complex. Overall, the article argued, "Catholic colleges weigh light on the U.S. academic scales. There is no

Catholic equivalent of Amherst, Oberlin, Reed or Swarthmore, let alone Harvard, Yale or Princeton. Notre Dame itself is not yet among the top schools."[29]

In his interview for *Time*, Hesburgh chose to see this criticism of Catholic schools as an opportunity. The flip side of past failure is future promise, the flip side of leaving mediocrity is entering excellence. Hesburgh took exception to George Bernard Shaw's quip that "a Catholic university is a contradiction in terms," instead arguing that both secure faith and free inquiry, together, enhance the education of the whole person. Displaying his confidence in the harmony of faith and reason, he argued that the rigor of scientific investigation is not hampered by Notre Dame's Catholic commitments: "There is no conflict between science and theology except where there is bad science or bad theology."

Catholic universities have a unique mission to bridge the gap between these two realms, and they needed to step up to the task: "We must somehow match secular or state universities in their comprehension of a vast spectrum of natural truths in the arts and sciences, while at the same time we must be in full possession of our own true heritage of theological wisdom."[30] In this work of mediating between seemingly disparate camps, the university must remember that it is, first and foremost, an intellectual enterprise. Piety is no substitute for competence. As important as its *Catholic* identity is and must continue to be, a Catholic university is a *university* first.

To achieve his goal of transforming Notre Dame into a great Catholic university, Hesburgh announced an historic capital campaign the year he became president. The "Program for the Future" set out to raise $66 million over ten years. In 1960, Hesburgh hit the jackpot when the Ford Foundation selected Notre Dame as one of only six universities to receive a $6 million challenge grant. Just to be among this elite group of schools, which included Johns Hopkins, Vanderbilt, Denver, Brown, and Stanford, was itself a ringing endorsement of Hesburgh's vision. But the lasting impact of the grant was the way it cranked Notre Dame's fundraising operation into high gear. The award stipulated that each school raise an additional $12 million in matching funds within three years. Notre Dame quickly surpassed that goal, bringing in over $18 million in cash gifts by 1963. Over the next decade, subsequent drives would raise $22 million ("Challenge II") and $62.5 million ("SUMMA")—far surpassing Hesburgh's original, ambitious goal.

Hesburgh's first major fundraising initiative was clearly, and unsurprisingly, focused on academic improvement. The money would support faculty development, student aid, housing for graduate students, and research facilities. The centerpiece was a new library, which Hesburgh saw as both a practical necessity and a symbolic statement of Notre Dame's commitment to academic greatness. The old library was bursting at the seams, overwhelmed by a university that had grown five times in size since the library opened in 1917. Lemmonier Library (now Bond Hall) was antiquated and inadequate to the needs of a modern research university. An editorial in the Notre Dame *Scholastic* complained about the difficulty of checking out materials. "Most students ordering books from the card catalogue have often wondered if that index was a list of books the University had or wanted to buy."[31]

Early plans for the new Memorial Library imagined a glistening modern structure at the heart of campus. Since his time overseeing construction projects as executive vice president, Hesburgh was committed to the idea that "form follows function." In the past, he grumbled, "architects would draw up a beautiful Gothic exterior for the size building needed, and only later would someone try to figure out how best to make it functional."[32] Hesburgh didn't want to look back; he wanted to look forward. However, some of the first designs for the new library were frighteningly futuristic—with a cube-shaped, glass complex replacing the historic Administration Building, its golden dome preserved only by suspending it in space atop a narrow obelisk.

Given the inevitable uproar from alumni such a move would ignite, planners instead settled for a spot on the edge of campus, east of the fieldhouse and just north of the stadium, on the very spot where Hesburgh had spent his first years as a priest ministering to the families of Vetville. The glass cube was replaced with a buff-colored brick and stone tower fourteen stories tall. The final design reflected the two-fold purpose of the building. The sprawling, two-story base would house the College Library, catering mainly to undergraduates. The tower would house the Research Library, containing more specialized resources for graduate students and faculty.

To break the monotony of the neutral Mankato stone that ran up this skyscraper of a library, Notre Dame commissioned an enormous mural of Christ, the Word of Life, constructed as a mosaic by the California artist Millard Sheets out of more than six thousand pieces of colored granite. The original hope was for the mural to face west, toward Sacred Heart Church, the Administration Building, and the center of campus. However, when it became clear that the old fieldhouse would block the view of the mural, the architects rotated the building to the south, so that Christ, with arms extended overhead in blessing, now looked down on the football stadium. The library was dedicated in May of 1964. But before the first snap of the first game that fall, the Notre

Dame Memorial Library had already been christened by students and fans, "Touchdown Jesus."

"Thinking of this as 'Touchdown Jesus' was just not in my mind or anybody else's for that matter," Hesburgh later said. "I had no idea of [the mural's] juxtaposition with the stadium; it never crossed my mind."[33] Though it is hard today to imagine missing the connection, the library was turned not to face the stadium, in fact, but to front a new academic quadrangle that stretched out between the two. As the Memorial Library was going up, two other buildings appeared just south of it, a new radiation laboratory and a computer center—both designed in a stark, modernist style. In 1967, Galvin Life Science Center was added to the quad.

To the north of the library, campus architects laid out plans for a space-age residential area ("Mod Quad"), with high-rise dormitories surrounding a futuristic chapel whose swirling conch shell exterior could have housed a ride at Disneyworld. (The chapel never materialized, and only Grace and Flanner Towers were ever constructed.)

Thus the new library sat at the center of the "new Notre Dame" that Hesburgh imagined—dynamic, state-of-the-art, academically rigorous, scientifically sophisticated, and thoroughly modern. The new Notre Dame had to be all these things, while at the same time maintaining its deeply Catholic character. Although Hesburgh embraced "Touchdown Jesus" as "a nice, friendly, familiar name for this beautiful piece of art," the nickname obscures the way in which the library and its famous mural sum up in stone Hesburgh's vision of a modern Catholic university.

A great Catholic university, Hesburgh repeated again and again, had to be both *Catholic* and a *university*. It had to be both ancient and new, religious and modern, faithful and rational, committed and curious. The Catholic university's real contribution—its vocation—was to mediate between two worlds that were too often held apart, to the impoverishment of both. This is how Hesburgh saw his own priestly ministry to mediate between heaven and earth. It is how he saw the priestly role of the laity who stand with a foot in both church and world. It is how he saw the priestly function of the university to draw together academic exploration and committed belief. Like many Catholics of his generation, Hesburgh was inspired by the sea change brought about by the Second Vatican Council (1962–65), with its emphasis on the church's engagement with the modern world. By affixing a 132-foot image of Christ to the proudly modernist exterior of his library, Hesburgh proclaimed that ancient faith and modern reason, together, were the one mission of a great Catholic university.

The inspiration for this bold architectural statement came to Hesburgh on a 1955 tour of the recently completed Central Library at the Universidad Nacional Autónoma de México (UNAM) in Mexico City. That library was designed by the noted Mexican artist Juan O'Gorman as a ten-story windowless block covered in colored tile mosaics. These murals present a symbolic retelling of Mexican history. As a kind of "showpiece of the Mexican government's achievements in modernizing the country," the art is decidedly anticolonial (and thus anti-Catholic) in spirit, privileging Mexico's pre-Christian past and its post-Revolution present.[34] The preponderance of Aztec gods covering the library led Hesburgh to complain about the "paganistic outlook" of the murals. More troubling for Hesburgh, however, was the antithetical relationship implied between faith and science.

The library's most famous mural narrates Mexico's colonial era. The Christian notions of good and evil are envisioned as two circles that, from a distance, become the eyes of the Aztec god Tlaloc. One circle depicts Ptolemy placing the earth at the center of the universe, the other portrays Copernicus with the sun at the center. According to O'Gorman's depiction, the Christian conquistadors saw Ptolemy as "the good, faith," while Copernicus represented "the bad, science." According to art historian Margaret Grubiak, "In casting the Spanish—and by extension Catholic—worldview as good versus bad and faith versus science on a university campus, O'Gorman portrayed an inimical relationship between Catholicism and academic inquiry, which was exactly the kind of relationship the University of Notre Dame wished to counter."[35]

Hesburgh made clear to donors and designers that he wanted the Word of Life mural to serve as a counterpoint to the Mexico City mural. "At its founding in 1910, UNAM was made a public university separate from the control of the Catholic Church in order to allow greater academic freedom. In his work at Notre Dame, Hesburgh strove to show that academic freedom and a Catholic identity could indeed coexist and thrive together."[36]

Rather than the mask of a pagan god, the unifying feature of Sheets' composition would be the cross, out of which rises Christ, arms outstretched. Fifty-one unnamed men surround Christ. They represent the procession of human knowledge, clustered into groups of figures from the Old Testament, the Eastern world, the medieval era, and ancient classical cultures (lower register); the Renaissance, the age of science, and the Byzantine era (middle register); the apostles and Christians of the early church (upper register). Unfortunately, no women were included among these exemplary models of faith and scholarship—an omission that reflects the institutional bias of the all-male school. Angles of light radiate from Christ, illuminating this "never-ending line of great scholars, thinkers, and teachers" leading up to the great teacher, the Word of Life, Jesus. "The mural articulated for the University of Notre Dame a mission statement for the modern Catholic university, sanctioning academic freedom with the awareness and belief that Christ is its center and ultimate aim."[37] It is hard to imagine a better depiction of Hesburgh's worldview—a vision of excellence rooted in faith and engaged in the world.

CHAPTER FOUR

Serving the World

Later in life Hesburgh admitted, "I'd have been bored to death if all I did was be the president of the university."[1] During his thirty-five years at the helm of Notre Dame, Hesburgh ventured off campus to engage some of the most pressing challenges of his day. He served on the National Science Board at the height of the Cold War. He served on the US Civil Rights Commission through the turmoil of the sixties. He served on the Presidential Clemency Board in the aftermath of Vietnam. Hesburgh accepted a total of sixteen presidential appointments and dozens of other assignments. He helped launch the Peace Corps under Kennedy and worked to reform immigration long before Reagan. In November of 1979, columnist Colman McCarthy wryly observed, "For a few perilous moments last month the federal government was left dangling without the services of the Rev. Theodore Hesburgh. When his work on the President's commission on the Holocaust ended, a full 48 hours passed before he was appointed to head the Commission on Immigration and Refugee Policy."[2] Ubiquitous in his black clerics and white Roman collar, Father Hesburgh stood as a priest on the American stage, embodying a kind of civic and moral leadership rarely seen before and rarely seen since.

Alongside his service to country, Hesburgh took on an exhausting array of other commitments around the world. As president of the International Federation of Catholic Universities from 1963 to 1970, he led that organization through historic change. As Vatican representative to the International Atomic Energy Agency, he facilitated dialogue between American and Soviet scientists. For eleven years as chair of the Overseas Development Council, and for twenty-one years on the board of the Rockefeller Foundation, Hesburgh oversaw millions of dollars in aid to developing nations. He visited over 130 countries during his career, giving rise to the famous joke back on campus: "What's the difference between God and Father Hesburgh? God is everywhere. Father Hesburgh is everywhere *but* Notre Dame."

Hesburgh would bristle at the implication that he was inattentive to the university he loved. His external engagements, he believed, contributed to the prominence of Notre Dame and fostered partnerships that benefitted the institution. Besides, Hesburgh would argue, a president not worth seeing outside the university was not worth seeing inside it.

Hesburgh did not say yes to everything. His outside commitments almost always had a moral dimension, and he frequently found himself speaking out for broader humane values. Yet, there was something deeper to Hesburgh's desire to engage the world, and it was rooted in his understanding of his own priestly ministry. For Hesburgh, a priest was first and foremost a mediator—called not only to span the gap between God and humanity, but also to build bridges between human beings. Driving his breakneck schedule and his varied engagements was a consistent and passionate desire to bring people together.

Nowhere was this zeal for reconciliation more evident than in Hesburgh's fifteen years of service on the US Civil Rights Commission. When he accepted President Dwight Eisenhower's invitation in 1957 to join the newly created body, Hesburgh knew that his involvement would not be popular with Notre Dame's conservative white alumni. Yet he threw himself into the work, arguing vigorously that racial justice was not just a civil right, but a moral imperative demanded by the very Catholic commitments that Notre Dame sought to instill.

At the time of his appointment, Hesburgh would have been an unlikely champion for racial justice. Prior to 1957, Hesburgh had little to do with the emerging civil rights movement. He read about the fierce resistance to *Brown v. Board of Education*, the 1954 Supreme Court decision ruling school segregation unconstitutional, and he followed the year-long Montgomery Bus Boycott, but from a distance. Hesburgh supported modest efforts toward integration at Notre Dame in the 1950s, but he dedicated no special energy to it, and few students of color enrolled. Clearly, in his early quest for academic excellence, Hesburgh saw other changes as more pressing.

Ironically, it may have been Hesburgh's reputation as a trustworthy national figure who was *not* particularly engaged on civil rights that led to his appointment to the commission in the first place. When Eisenhower signed the 1957 Civil Rights Act—the first civil rights legislation since Reconstruction—few had high hopes. Thanks largely to the Senate Majority Leader from Texas, Lyndon Johnson, the bill survived its winding way through Congress but emerged as a weak piece of compromise legislation. However, buried in the bill was the establishment of a six-member Commission on Civil Rights, which was to act as an independent, bipartisan agency charged to investigate alleged instances of voter suppression and other violations of equal protection under the law. It was a fact-finding agency, with no enforcement powers and no clear mandate for change, other than to study the situation and make recommendations. Ike's assistant Sherman Adams recruited a group of former governors and academic leaders to serve on the commission, men who reflected Eisenhower's moderate approach to civil rights—three Democrats, two Republicans, and one political independent, Father Hesburgh.

At the president's request, the commission was split between three northerners (John Hannah, Ernest Wilkins, and Hesburgh) and three southerners (John Battle, Robert Storey, and Doyle Carlton), which seemed to set the group up for a stalemate. Commentators were skeptical. Given commission members' lack of experience with the civil rights movement, and their "devotion to the cause of moderation," one editorial predicted that they were "not likely to break many lances crusading for civil rights."[3]

Hesburgh, however, saw greater potential. After the commission's first meeting in January 1958, Hesburgh reached out to a young DC lawyer named Harris Wofford and asked if they could meet up in Lafayette Park, right in front of the White House. Wofford had written a memo shortly after the passage of the 1957 Civil Rights Act, proposing steps the newly created commission might take to address the racial impasse. Hesburgh read the memo and wanted to talk. Wofford later recalled being impressed "that a busy executive would initiate a meeting with an unknown author of a memorandum simply because he is interested in the writer's ideas." Hesburgh asked Wofford, "Now that you see who the members are, do you still think the Commission can do something important?" As they walked and talked, Wofford began to wonder out loud whether the North-South division in the commission might be turned into an asset. "Could the divided Commission provide the missing dialogue at the highest level that the racial problem required?"[4]

Hesburgh embraced Wofford and his suggestion whole-heartedly. He invited the young lawyer to serve as his legal counsel on the commission and later tried to recruit him to help create a civil rights center at the Notre Dame law school. Hesburgh made every effort to build relationships with the other commissioners. He and John Hannah, the president of Michigan State University and chairman of the commission, quickly established rapport, often seeing eye-to-eye on issues.

More challenging was John Battle, the former governor of Virginia and the most outspoken segregationist on the commission. The son of a Protestant minister, Battle did not quite know what to make of the Catholic priest—although the two men did share a taste for bourbon. Hesburgh began to bring a bottle along whenever the commission met (or leave Battle a message when it was his turn). They often shared a glass after the day's work was done, talking late into the night about family, religion, and politics.[5]

Observing Hesburgh at close range, Wofford came to see in him "a man of curiosity, compassion, conviction, and courage." Although at the beginning Hesburgh "seemed quite conservative," Wofford found him "[o]pen-minded, warm, and direct . . . a promising participant in any dialogue." Wofford concluded that Hesburgh's approach was "to reach and reason with a person, not to manipulate or defeat him."[6]

If Hesburgh had little experience with issues surrounding racial discrimination prior to his appointment, he neverthe-less recognized the moral importance of the commission's work from the start. In an interview with the *South Bend Tribune*, he said he would approach his task in the "moral knowledge that all men are created equal." He believed that time would eventually cure the sickness of discrimination, but, he added, "we may have to nudge time a bit."[7] Although he started out cautious, Hesburgh became increasingly outspoken on civil rights. His experience on the commission would prove a decisive turning point in his career—transforming him from a concerned citizen into a lifelong advocate for racial justice.

The commission was sworn in on January 3, 1958. Thanks to delaying tactics by Southerners in the Senate, the commission was not confirmed until March. They did not hold their first hearings until December—almost a full year into their two-year term. The commission encountered one obstacle after another. They could not secure hotel reservations in Montgomery because three members of their team (Commissioner Wilkins and two staff attorneys) were black, and all the hotels were segregated. When they asked for lodging at Maxwell Air Force Base, the commanding officer refused, saying that the people of Montgomery would not stand for housing whites and blacks in the same barracks. After both the Secretary of the Air Force and the Secretary of Defense refused to override the decision of the local commander, Hannah called the president. According to Hesburgh, "Ike blew a fuse." The former five-star general issued an executive order overturning the commander's decision.

When the commission requested county voting records, the local circuit judge (and future Alabama governor) George Wallace refused, impounding the registration files and declaring publicly, "I will jail any Civil Rights Commission agent who attempts to get the records."[8] During the first day of hearings, one local official after another failed to cooperate, feigning ignorance or simply refusing to answer questions. The contemptuous defiance of the commission drew harsh rebuke in newspaper editorials across the country. Eisenhower called the conduct of the Alabama officials "reprehensible."[9] Even Southerners who were critical of the commission found the display embarrassing and counterproductive.

Hesburgh and his fellow commissioners did hear from black witnesses who testified to the systematic effort by local officials to deprive them of the right to vote. The first morning of hearings, some twenty-six African Americans took the stand—all were well-educated professionals, many graduates of Tuskegee Institute, who worked as teachers, doctors, or civil service employees. Some had been registered voters in other states before moving to Alabama; all met the age, residency, and other legal requirements for voting. Yet, in each case, local registration boards found ways to reject their applications.

Their stories were strikingly similar: First, they had great difficulty finding out when and where they would be allowed to register; usually it was one day a month in some remote location. Only one or two applications would be considered at a time, so they had to wait outside in long lines, often for several hours. Once admitted to the room, applicants endured a lengthy process that included copying out a specific article of the Constitution and completing a long and complicated form. A single misspelling or missing date could be grounds for rejecting the entire application.

Over the course of two days, commission members grew increasingly sympathetic to their African American witnesses, despite the commission's best efforts to maintain a stance of impartiality. After hearing from a black farmer who had tried and failed to register on multiple occasions, Hesburgh asked him, "Mr. Sellers, are you going to keep trying?" When the man said, "Oh, yes, I'm determined to register," Hesburgh broke protocol by responding, "God bless you."[10]

After Alabama, the commission moved on to hold hearings in Texas, Georgia, Mississippi, and Louisiana. Everywhere the story was the same. Over the course of several months, the commission and its staff compiled a mountain of evidence demonstrating, beyond the shadow of a doubt, that in states across the South, black citizens were being deliberately and systematically denied their right to vote solely on the basis of race. They also gathered damning data on discrimination in public education and housing. Chairman John Hannah worked slowly and deliberatively to forge a broad consensus between the Northerners and the Southerners on the commission. Yet, as they began work on their final report, differences remained, particularly on what role the federal government should play in protecting voting rights.

When Hesburgh arrived in Shreveport, Louisiana, in July of 1959, for the final public hearing of the commission, he was met by a federal marshal informing him that there would be no hearing because a federal judge had declared it unconstitutional. While the staff filed an appeal (the Supreme Court ultimately upheld the commission's right to meet), commission members faced the prospect of three days stuck on an Air Force base—crammed into stifling rooms, fed terrible food, and kept up all night by the sound of jet engines. In his autobiography, Hesburgh wrote, "We were a dejected group of people, commiserating with one another and wondering 'What do we do now?'"[11] Their report to the president and Congress was due in a few weeks, and they still had to decide on final recommendations; but the prospect of working in the heat and humidity only further demoralized them.

Hesburgh proposed a change in venue. Borrowing a private plane from Notre Dame's legendary benefactor, I. A. O'Shaughnessy, Hesburgh flew the whole commission to northern Wisconsin, where the university owned a seven-thousand-acre retreat property. The camp at Land O'Lakes was one of Hesburgh's favorite places, where he often went to relax, recharge, and, above all, fish. In fact, as they made their way north, the six commissioners discovered an important fact. Despite sharp disagreements over segregation, states' rights, and federal oversight, they all shared something in common: Every one of them loved to fish.

The commissioners spent the afternoon on the lake, reeling in a good number of bass and walleye, while the rest of the staff worked away on the final report. "When it got too dark to continue fishing," Hesburgh recounted, "we gathered around a big table on the screened porch. Everyone was feeling very mellow because of the great fishing, the driest martinis, and a great dinner."[12]

One of the staff members, Berl Bernhard, recognized how Hesburgh played a very shrewd host. Earlier that day, Hesburgh had put Battle in the same boat as the new black commissioner, George Johnson, who joined the commission after the sudden death of Ernest Wilkins. Hesburgh's goal was to develop rapport between the two men on opposite sides of the segregation issue. "It was all calculated," observed Bernhard. "It gave the appearance of casual fun, but it had a purpose . . . to accomplish as great a unanimity as was possible."[13]

Following the meal, the staff presented the commissioners with twelve recommendations for their vote. Hesburgh's assistant Harris Wofford recalled, "There was a full moon over the lake, and an after-dinner glow on the Commissioners when they decided to take up the most controversial recommendations first."[14] According to Hesburgh, "The results of the vote exceeded the expectations of even the hardiest optimists among us."[15] Eleven of the recommendations passed unanimously. The twelfth passed five-to-one. Battle dissented from the group's recommendation to appoint temporary federal registrars to register voters, which he saw as federal overreach. Hannah, Johnson, and Hesburgh wanted to see the government go even further. They included a "proposal" for a constitutional amendment to guarantee universal suffrage. The three men also went beyond the commission's unanimous recommendations regarding education by proposing that colleges and universities be required to demonstrate nondiscrimination as a condition for receiving federal funds.[16]

When the commission presented their report to the president in September of 1959, Eisenhower was astounded that three Northerners and three Southerners could find so much common ground. "It's because we're all fishermen," Hesburgh said. To which Ike famously replied, "Then we need more fishermen!"[17]

There is some wisdom in this good-natured exchange. By no means did the 1959 report reflect perfect unanimity. But the success of the commission was due, in large part, to the relationships built among its members. Their work confirmed Hesburgh's conviction that people of good will can come together to resolve even the most intractable differences. Just a few months after delivering the report, Hesburgh told participants at a civil rights conference that one of the most amazing things about the experience was that the commissioners all became very close friends. "I think we developed for each other the kind of compatibility and understanding, and even perhaps at times compassion, that was a necessary ingredient in any kind of fruitful solution to this very vexing problem."[18]

For Hesburgh, the experience of the commission transcended collegiality and individual friendships; it transcended legal theories and legislation. The whole question of civil rights was, for Hesburgh, "first and foremost and fundamentally a theological problem, a moral problem, a spiritual problem."[19] At its heart was the "sacred reality" of the human person. Through their hearings, site visits, and other investigations, the members of the commission encountered black Americans face-to-face. They saw their suffering up close and recognized their courage. "These weren't units to us," Hesburgh explained. "They were flesh and blood people."[20]

In a personal statement appended to the 1959 report, Hesburgh laid out the philosophical and theological convictions that guided his work on the commission: "I believe that civil rights were not created, but only recognized and formulated, by our Federal and State constitutions and charters. Civil rights are important corollaries of the great proposition, at the heart of Western civilization, that every human person is a *res sacra*, a sacred reality, and as such is entitled to the opportunity of fulfilling those great human potentials with which God has endowed every man."[21]

A month after delivering their report to the president, Hesburgh spoke at the Catholic Interracial Council Communion Breakfast in Chicago. The setting allowed him to elaborate on his *theological* commitment to civil rights, which he saw as a commitment flowing directly out of the teachings of the Catholic Church. Hesburgh talked about the unity of the human race that comes from Adam and Eve. He pointed to Christ's saving death for all of humanity, without exception. He explained that the very word "Catholic" means "universal and comprising all, excluding none."

He then told the story of meeting a wealthy white woman at a fundraiser who was amazed to hear that Notre Dame admitted black students. When Hesburgh asked why she was amazed, she replied, "Well, Notre Dame is too good for Negroes."

Hesburgh responded gently, "Just let your mind run for a moment. What is the best place there is?"

"Well, I suppose you're talking about heaven," she answered.

Hesburgh asked, "Do you think there are any Negroes in heaven?"

She said, "I never thought of it. . . . Well . . . Yes, I guess there must be Negroes in heaven."

"I suppose you want to go there?" Hesburgh continued. She said, "Yes."

"Well," Hesburgh concluded, "maybe you'd better get started thinking a little bit about living with Negroes on earth, so you will be ready for heaven."[22]

Hesburgh argued that those Catholics who were opposed to civil rights for African Americans were "about as anachronistic as a dinosaur." How could so many good people, "so generous to good causes, so personable in their family life, so faithful to their wives, so loving to their children" be so unconcerned and so wrong about issues of "social morality"? They hadn't caught up to their church! "They are completely out of step with the mind of Christ and the mind of the Church, the word of the Encyclicals, the letters of the Bishops—the basic Catholic doctrine."[23] The parable of the Good Samaritan tells us that our neighbor is the person in difficulty. The Last Judgment scene in Matthew's Gospel reveals that whatever we do for the least of our brothers and sisters, we do for Christ. Hesburgh told his Catholic audience that he was convinced that the case for civil rights, "as I've given it to you dogmatically, is founded upon the Catholic faith."[24]

The widespread religiosity of the 1950s and the post-war mainstreaming of American Catholics made it possible for Hesburgh to weave his distinctively Catholic commitments seamlessly into the language of American civil religion. Speaking to the American Academy of Arts and Sciences, Hesburgh said that, while serving on the Civil Rights Commission, when debate got tense or consensus seemed impossible, one of the staff would slip him a note scribbled on a legal pad that read: "Better give them some theology." We may disagree on all manner of things, Hesburgh told the audience, but ultimately, "anyone who understands anything of the Judeo-Christian tradition at the base of Western Culture must hold some common principles about the nature and destiny of man which alone validate the society in which we live."[25]

This unqualified appeal to a common "Judeo-Christian" heritage reflects a fundamental assumption about the compatibility of the "city of God" and the "city of man," to borrow Saint Augustine's famous distinction. Hesburgh saw no inherent contradiction between the revealed tenets of his faith and the founding principles of his country. But he was clear: where conflict might arise between the two, one's conscience overruled the law of the land.

Hesburgh's insistence on the primacy of the transcendent over the temporal, and his refusal to relegate religion to one's private life, stood at odds with the priorities of another prominent Catholic of his generation, John F. Kennedy. Hesburgh knew Jack Kennedy long before he was elected president. Father John Cavanaugh, Hesburgh's mentor at Notre Dame, was a close friend and frequent house guest of Joe Kennedy, the patriarch of the Kennedy clan. When Hesburgh became president, he followed Cavanaugh's lead and reached out to the Kennedys, inviting members of the family to sit on various councils and advisory boards at the university. Hesburgh even took up a special assignment from Joe in 1953, meeting with his daughter Eunice, who wanted to become a nun, in order to encourage her to marry her suitor, Sargent Shriver.[26] Hesburgh had great respect for "Sarge," as did Eunice, who finally accepted his proposal.

It was through his good friend Sargent Shriver that Hesburgh was drawn into one of the most rewarding projects of his career. During his 1960 campaign for president, Kennedy proposed a bold and inspiring idea: a "Peace Corps" of young Americans who would enlist for two years of service in the developing world. Hesburgh thought it was "brilliant . . . just the kind of thing this country needed."[27] Shortly after the inauguration, Kennedy put Shriver in charge, ably assisted by Harris Wofford, who had left Hesburgh's side at the Civil Rights Commission in order to work on Kennedy's campaign. The two men asked Hesburgh for help. He threw himself into the project, energized and inspired by the response. Hesburgh wrote to Shriver, "We may take some comfort and pride in the fact that the general softness and selfishness of so many of our elders have not been able to extinguish the native idealism, the generosity, and the pioneering spirit of our young people."[28]

With Notre Dame's ties in South America, the group chose Chile for the pilot project. In collaboration with the Indiana Conference of Higher Education, Notre Dame served as the program host. On July 20, 1961, fifty-two volunteers arrived on campus for a ten-week orientation. Hesburgh played an active role, personally welcoming the volunteers, arranging a picnic at Lake Michigan, and checking in on the group regularly. The first week, one young woman wrote home, "Father Hesburgh appears to be a very forward-thinking man and also one who understands young people."[29] Forty-five volunteers left for Chile that fall and, in the spring, Hesburgh wrote to Walter Langford, the program director, to say that he was coming to Chile for seven days in April, and that he wanted to visit all forty-five of the volunteers.

"It's impossible," Langford replied, the volunteers were spread out over eight hundred miles, scattered in remote areas. It would take over a month.

"Impossible or not," Hesburgh answered, "we've got to do it. I can't see some of them without seeing all of them."[30]

Hesburgh did it. Traveling by plane, train, bus, and jeep, he was able to inspect all of the placement sites, delivering to each volunteer a signed letter from President Kennedy thanking them for their service. Once back in the United States, Hesburgh personally contacted the parents of each volunteer, reporting on their work and relaying messages home.

Notre Dame continued its work with the Peace Corps for five years, helping to get the program off the ground. During this time, Hesburgh remained actively engaged on the Civil Rights Commission. President Eisenhower appreciated the work of the original commission but did little to act on their recommendations, other than to ensure the agency would be renewed for another two-year term. After JFK was elected, it quickly became clear that civil rights was not high on the new administration's agenda. Hesburgh attributed Kennedy's reluctance to move aggressively on civil rights to the president's fear of antagonizing voters in the South, whom he would need for reelection. It was a political calculus that deeply disappointed Hesburgh.

By 1962, the Civil Rights Commission was feeling stymied by the Kennedy administration and found itself increasingly at odds with the president's forceful attorney general, his brother Bobby. Some of Hesburgh's own impatience can already be heard in the statement that he attached to the commission's second report to Congress in 1961. As a reporter for the *New York Times* put it, there "one man's indignation over man's inhumanity to man burst into vivid words."[31] Hesburgh bemoaned the continued resistance of so many Americans to progress on civil rights. "Why does America, the foremost bastion of democracy, demonstrate at home so much bitter evidence of the utter disregard for human dignity that we are contesting on so many fronts abroad?"[32] He reiterated his view that belief in the "sacredness" of the human person was the central basis of the "magnificent theory" undergirding the American dream. He pointed to the report itself—five large volumes cataloging ongoing discrimination in voting, education, employment, housing, and the administration of justice—and concluded that this theory just wasn't working. "Inherent in the depressing story is the implication that it is not working because we really do not believe in man's inner dignity and rightful aspiration to equality—unless he happens to be a white man."

In the statement's most often quoted passage, the lifelong aviation buff took aim at the priorities of the new Catholic president: "Personally, I don't care if the United States gets the first man on the moon, if while this is happening on a crash basis we dawdle along here on our corner of the earth, nursing our prejudices, flouting our magnificent Constitution, ignoring the central moral problem of our times, and appearing hypocrites to all the world."[33]

Hesburgh had come to see the Civil Rights Commission as "a kind of national conscience in the matter of civil rights" and, increasingly, as "a burr under the saddle of the administration." Bobby Kennedy saw it as "a runaway grand jury that might suddenly at a critical juncture propose something he didn't want proposed."[34] As attorney general, he claimed oversight of civil rights and did not like the independence and political indifference of the commission. Three times in 1962 he forced the commission to postpone scheduled hearings in Mississippi. He said he wanted to avoid compromising federal anti-discrimination cases being brought by the

Justice Department, but Hesburgh saw a failure of nerve on the part of the administration to take on the white power structure in the South. According to William Taylor, one of the staff members, "Fr. Hesburgh was among the most stalwart, if not the most stalwart, person of the Commission." Hesburgh told the other commissioners, "We must do what's right in these circumstances. We are here not to please any particular president, but to do a job of exposing conditions."[35]

Both the president and his brother respected Hesburgh, but they thought he was causing unnecessary trouble. Bobby, losing patience, complained to colleagues, "And then there was always Father Hesburgh coming around the corner telling me what I was doing wrong."[36]

The delays angered Hesburgh and the others. By March 1963, the commissioners "were incensed that their silent submission to the Administration had stretched into a shameful record of complicity."[37] They decided to issue a report without the Mississippi hearings, basing their conclusions on staff research. Their April 16 statement condemned police brutality, intimidation, and other repressive measures designed to prevent blacks from voting in the state of Mississippi. It came at a tense turning point in the civil rights struggle. That same month, Martin Luther King, Jr., and the Southern Christian Leadership Conference brought their nonviolent protest to Birmingham, Alabama, where King himself was arrested. There he wrote his famous "Letter from a Birmingham Jail," excoriating those "white churchmen" who "stand on the sideline and mouth pious irrelevancies and sanctimonious trivialities."[38]

Hesburgh did not know King well, nor did he join the protests that spread rapidly across the South in the late 1950s and early 1960s. But he had great respect for the civil rights leader and admired the August 28, 1963, March on Washington, where King gave his great "I Have a Dream" speech. The following year, at a June 1964 civil rights rally at Soldier Field in Chicago, Hesburgh was invited onto the dais with King, gave an impromptu speech, and then linked arms with the civil rights leader as the entire platform party, along with 50,000 rally participants, all sang "We Shall Overcome."

While Hesburgh and the other commissioners labored away documenting discrimination, television brought into American living rooms shocking images of white police officers unleashing dogs and leveling fire hoses against young African Americans demonstrating peacefully. The constant stream of news stories covering the protests in cities across the South finally forced Kennedy to speak out, which he did in a June 11, 1963, address to the nation, in which he called on Congress to pass a new civil rights bill. However, the young president's tragic death on November 22 left the fate of that legislation—as it left so much—unfinished.

Whatever concern Hesburgh may have had about the future of the Civil Rights Commission soon disappeared as Lyndon Johnson assumed the presidency. In his first speech to Congress, Johnson said that he wanted to honor Kennedy's legacy by passing the civil rights bill he had proposed. In February 1964 the commission met with the president. They were squeezed in between appointments at the end of a long day, and Johnson looked exhausted. He suggested they move to a smaller room off the Oval Office where he could stretch out on a couch. The president confirmed his commitment to civil rights, but what most struck Hesburgh was Johnson's sincerity when it came to the problem of poverty. After Hesburgh suggested that the president's poverty program be framed more positively by, for example, renaming it the "equal opportunity" program, Johnson spoke at length about Franklin D. Roosevelt and all that he did to lift people out of poverty. "When I'm dead and gone," he said, "all I want to be said of my presidency is that there were fewer poor people at the end of it than there were at the beginning."[39]

On July 2, 1964, President Lyndon Johnson signed the landmark Civil Rights Act into law. Hesburgh saw the moment as vindication of the seven years of hard work he had invested in the commission. He gave LBJ much of the credit for passage of the Civil Rights Act as well as the Voting Rights Act of 1965 and the Fair Housing Act of 1968. "I don't think Jack Kennedy, had he lived, could have done it."[40] He saw a ruthlessness in the Southerner turned toward a good end.

Hesburgh was proud of the service he had provided to his country. And two days after the bill was signed, Hesburgh learned that he would receive the Presidential Medal of Freedom in recognition of his contribution. At the award ceremony that September, Hesburgh stood among the nation's elite. He was the youngest recipient in a group that included such major American figures as Aaron Copland, Walt Disney, Lena F. Edwards, T. S. Eliot, Helen Keller, John L. Lewis, Edward R. Murrow, Reinhold Niebuhr, Carl Sandburg, John Steinbeck, and Helen Taussig.

At times, Hesburgh's positive assessment of the 1960s civil rights legislation bordered on the Pollyannaish, giving the impression that discrimination against African Americans vanished overnight. "One day blacks were barred from a lot of places. The next day they were not." Obviously, he acknowledged, "all the problems of racial inequality have not been solved, but apartheid in the United States disappeared forever with the passage of that law in 1964 and it will never come back."[41] The fact that Hesburgh continued to serve on the Civil Rights Commission through 1972—until he was forced to resign by President Richard Nixon—suggests Hesburgh had a keen sense and a clear commitment to the work that still needed to be done. But his own perspective was very much shaped by his place on the commission, which determined not only what he saw, but also what he did not.

According to Michael O'Brien, "Fr. Ted himself often praised the Commission and President Johnson but almost invariably overlooked the dramatic impact of civil rights demonstrations like those in Birmingham (1963) and Selma (1965)."[42] In his autobiography, Hesburgh wrote: "The various 'wade-ins,' 'sit-ins,' and 'pray-ins' all helped the process along and the clincher, undoubtedly, was the persuasive power of the law. The most important factor, however, was the sense of fairness of the American people. Given the facts, they were ready to get rid of apartheid in this country."[43] It was as if he saw the civil rights struggles of the sixties not so much as a hard-fought battle, but as an exercise in public education.

In this later retrospective, there is a mellowing of Hesburgh's earlier rhetoric, which was often marked by a kind of "controlled moral indignation."[44] What remained constant was his fundamental theological commitment to the dignity of the human person, his faith in the "magnificent theory" of the American experiment, and his bedrock conviction that civil rights had to be a concern for every citizen. No American can escape taking a stand. "No American can really disengage himself from this problem. Each of us must choose to deepen the anguish of the problem, by silence and passivity, if nothing more, or must take a forthright stand on principles that give some hope of eventual solution."[45] As Hesburgh continued his work on the commission through the 1960s, he sought to illuminate the intricate intertwining of oppressions. Discrimination in education, housing, employment, and policing all combined to deny the rights of African Americans and other minorities, insulting the dignity with which they are endowed by their Creator.

Shortly after the election of Richard Nixon in 1968, Hesburgh, John Hannah, and other members of the commission made a courtesy call on the new president. As their meeting in the Oval Office wrapped up, Nixon asked Hesburgh to stay behind so that he could speak with him privately. The two men had known each other since November 1952, when the newly elected vice president and his wife visited Notre Dame for the USC game.

"What would it take for you to come full-time with the government?" Nixon asked Hesburgh. "Do I have to see the Pope?"[46]

This was not the first time Hesburgh had been approached about a career in government. In early 1968, the head of NASA, James Webb, had asked Hesburgh to take the place of Robert Seamans in the number two slot at the agency— with the implication that Hesburgh would succeed Webb when he retired.[47]

Nixon wasn't looking for Hesburgh to take over the space agency, but rather to head up the federal poverty program. Hesburgh demurred, and instead took the opportunity to advise Nixon on several weighty matters. He told the president that he needed to end the war in Vietnam, abolish the draft, give eighteen-year-olds the right to vote, and support a federal student loan program—all in the space of a few minutes! Hesburgh also suggested that it was time, after eleven long years, to step down from the Civil Rights Commission. The group needed new faces and fresh ideas, Hesburgh thought. Nixon listened attentively and said he would get back to him.

Instead of accepting Hesburgh's offer to step down, Nixon asked him to step up and serve as chair of the commission. Hesburgh agreed to do so for one year, in order to allow for transition to new leadership. However, it soon became clear to Hesburgh "that civil rights had few friends in the Nixon administration."[48]

Hesburgh sought to expand the purview of the commission beyond African Americans to include discrimination against Hispanics, Native Americans, and other minorities; he wanted to push forward into complex problems such as urban blight, busing, crime, and enforcement. The administration instead chose to pull back on the civil rights protections advanced under Johnson. Nixon's emerging "Southern strategy" targeted disaffected white voters, playing on racial resentment in order to draw Southern whites into the Republican camp.

At the end of his first year, Hesburgh decided to stay on as chair, feeling that he couldn't abandon the commission while it was under assault from the White House. Nixon was a friend, but that was not enough for Hesburgh to mute his criticism. "I don't believe in being friendly when it's a question of law or right or human dignity."[49] Under Hesburgh's leadership, the commission increasingly played the role of administration gadfly.

Just before the 1970 midterm elections, the Civil Rights Commission published its massive report on the federal government's compliance with its own anti-discrimination laws. The conclusion was damning. Of the forty departments and government agencies surveyed, all but one were judged to be "poor" in their enforcement of civil rights—the lowest rating possible. When Nixon's special assistant Len Garment got word of the report, he called Hesburgh. "My God," he said, "what are you trying to do to us?" He asked Hesburgh to delay releasing the report until after the election, in order to limit damage to the administration. Hesburgh refused, and even called a press conference to publicize the results. "The facts spoke for themselves," Hesburgh told Garment; "if the facts hurt, then the administration should get busy and do something to correct the causes."[50]

Hesburgh did not set out to embarrass the president, but the damage was done. As the Nixon team continued its civil rights strategy of benign neglect, Hesburgh became more and more critical of the administration's policies. By the end of Nixon's first term, the animosity of the administration toward the commission was intense. The infamous Nixon tapes recorded a conversation between the president and his two top aids, Bob Halderman and John Ehrlichman, in which the advisors complained about "the problem of Hesburgh," who was "always attacking us." They pressed to get rid of him or else "kill the Goddamn commission."[51] Nixon seemed convinced that Hesburgh had to go.

Meanwhile, in a speech at Union Theological Seminary in New York, Hesburgh laid out his most forceful critique to date, offering a searing indictment of America's failure to address the "color" issue. The *New York Times* published the speech on October 29, 1972, just one week before Nixon was overwhelmingly reelected President of the United States.[52] One week after the election, Nixon asked for Hesburgh's resignation from the Civil Rights Commission— a message that came through the secretary of an assistant to an advisor of the president—telling Hesburgh that he was to be out of his office by six o'clock that night.

"There was a spell of coldness between Nixon and me after I was sacked," Hesburgh recounted. "But when Watergate happened, I did not rejoice." Although he called Nixon's cohorts "a bunch of hucksters" in the wake of the scandal, Hesburgh refrained from publicly criticizing the president. And the two men made a kind of peace years later at a Hall of Fame dinner in New York. "As one gets older," Hesburgh reflected, "it becomes more apparent that forgiving and forgetting is much better than holding grudges. Besides, it is more Christian."[53]

CHAPTER FIVE

A Catholic University

In the fall of 1962, Hesburgh was immersed in his many commitments both on and off campus. In addition to serving on the Civil Rights Commission, the International Atomic Energy Agency, and several important boards, including the National Science Board and the Rockefeller Foundation, Hesburgh was busy leading a multi-million-dollar fundraising campaign, overseeing the construction of a new library, guiding the Peace Corps project, and responding to the first bursts of student unrest that would come to rock his tranquil campus. While he labored away for God, country, and Notre Dame, a religious event of historic proportions began to unfold in Rome that would soon affect virtually everything Hesburgh held dear.

The Second Vatican Council opened on October 11, 1962, with a magnificent ceremony in Saint Peter's Basilica that was broadcast to millions of viewers and covered by newspapers around the world. Some 2,500 bishops, cardinals, and other participants—joined by their advisors, official observers, dignitaries, and the press—gathered for a church event that had not been seen in a hundred years.

Just a few months into his pontificate, the round, smiling Pope John XXIII surprised even his closest advisors by announcing his desire to convene a worldwide (or "ecumenical") council. Unlike past ecumenical councils, Vatican II was not called to respond to some crisis or heresy. Rather, Pope John saw only opportunity—the opportunity to reach out to other Christians, to engage the modern world constructively, and to renew the life of the church. Arriving at the end of a long procession into the basilica, the aging pope knelt down at the main altar—under Michelangelo's dome and Bernini's bronze canopy—and formally opened the Second Vatican Council by intoning the hymn *Veni, Creator Spiritus*, "Come, Holy Spirit."[1]

That simple three-word prayer, "Come, Holy Spirit," was one of Hesburgh's favorites. The university president played no role at Vatican II, but he wholeheartedly embraced the course it set for the church. His deep Christian optimism resonated with the message of John XXIII's opening address, in which the pope called out those "prophets of gloom" around him who saw in modern times only "prevarication and ruin." Instead, Pope John believed, God was leading humanity to a new order of human relations. The church needed *aggiornamento*—"updating"—not because the church felt threatened, but because of its great desire to share Christ with all people. The pope pointed forward with hope: "The council now beginning rises in the church like daybreak, a forerunner of most splendid light. It is now only dawn."[2]

Although he did not use the word, *aggiornamento* was precisely what Hesburgh was trying to accomplish at Notre Dame. His quest for excellence demanded updating the tradition-bound university. It meant modern science and scholarship. It meant state-of-the-art facilities and cutting-edge research. It meant breaking out of a self-imposed ghetto

and engaging modern problems. It meant, above all, a bold-
ness to try what is new. "A new Ecumenical Council looms
before us," Hesburgh told an audience of Catholic educators
in 1961. In anticipation of that great event, he noted the
importance of dialogue between Protestant and Catholic
theologians in Europe, and then asked, "Why have we been
so timid here in our American institutions of higher learning? Must we always be the last to initiate anything imagi-
native and intellectual?"[3]

As he entered his second decade as president, Hesburgh
continued to press an agenda for change. "There is something almost sepulchral," he told the Council of Graduate
Schools in 1964, in the image of ivy-covered walls that universities like Notre Dame project. We live in a time of rapid
and fundamental change. Universities must actively partici-
pate in this process. Otherwise the broader societal transformation "is less likely to bear the ultimate marks of the
true and the good to which universities are by nature committed."[4] Their very dedication to the timeless pursuit of
truth not only liberates universities (particularly Catholic
universities) to adapt, but also qualifies them to guide, as-
sess, and critique adaptation itself.

Hesburgh complained about the tendency of Catholic
colleges and universities to rest on the laurels of an ancient
and rich tradition. While proudly claiming their seniority,
Catholics must avoid the vices of advanced age: "Spiteful
envy of other good efforts, the suspicious and almost instinc-
tive fear of youth and youthful ideas, the concrete fixation
with the status quo and the timid failure to respond to new
situations and the inevitable new challenges of every new
age."[5] Although he prized the enduring wisdom of the
Catholic tradition, Hesburgh had little patience with phi-
losophers and theologians nit picking among the problems

of the past. Too many pressing challenges faced humanity. "Personally, I have no ambition to be a mediaeval man," Hesburgh said. "Let the dead bury their dead."[6] Standing at the intersection of eternal truths and contemporary questions, the Catholic university must serve as mediator between change and the changeless. Instead of merely "holding to the tradition of what has been," Catholic educators must be "striving mightily to make the traditional values more relevant, more vital, more meaningful today."[7]

Of the many changes Hesburgh brought to Notre Dame, he identified two as the most consequential: the transfer of university governance to a predominantly lay board of trustees in 1967, and the admission of women as full-time undergraduates in 1972. The first decision largely came down from above; the second bubbled up from below.

Hesburgh estimated that when he became president in 1952, probably 95 percent of Notre Dame students were against coeducation. Fifteen years later, easily 95 percent were for it. The shift in sentiment extended far beyond Notre Dame, as a number of leading universities had already begun moving in this direction. Yale and Princeton admitted women in 1969, the same year that all-male Harvard and all-female Radcliffe formally began a long and painful merger process. When a similar attempt to merge with neighboring Saint Mary's College, run by the Holy Cross Sisters, fell apart, Notre Dame went ahead and admitted women on its own. In the fall of 1972, fifteen hundred women arrived to newly reconditioned residence halls and a "We're Glad You're Here" banner stretched across the front of South Dining Hall.

Hesburgh saw going coed as part of Notre Dame's quest for excellence. "In an era of rising sensitivities to rights and inequities, being single-sex was increasingly equated with being backward."[8] Hesburgh was always looking forward. Although he had an old-fashioned tendency to highlight the refining influence women would have on the men of Notre Dame, he understood the very real contributions these women were making to the academic life of the university. Admitting women automatically doubled the applicant pool, he liked to point out, which allowed Notre Dame to raise its admission standards even higher. And the new female students found in Hesburgh a strong advocate. Indeed, the fact that everybody—alumni and trustees, faculty and students—knew that Hesburgh wanted coeducation helped Notre Dame make the transition more smoothly than many of its peer institutions. But beyond his public position, Hesburgh's more private actions helped welcome women to campus. He attended their social events, presided at Mass in their dorms, took their concerns seriously, and engaged these new students as full and valued members of the university community.[9]

While Hesburgh played a supporting role in bringing women to Notre Dame, he took the lead in transferring control of the university from the Holy Cross order to a lay-led board of trustees. In his autobiography, Hesburgh drew a straight line from his doctoral thesis on the lay apostolate, through the Second Vatican Council, to the lay board at Notre Dame. Why turn the university over to the laity? For Hesburgh, the answer was simple: "Vatican II had said that laypeople should be given responsibility in Catholic affairs commensurate with their dedication, their competence, and their intelligence. Many people may not have taken that seriously, but we did. For me, it was the most natural thing in the world. In fact, I had advocated a greater role for the laity ever since I wrote my doctoral dissertation on the subject two decades earlier."[10]

Hesburgh's theological commitments may have given him an openness to lay leadership that other priest-presidents lacked; however, there were also very practical reasons for the change. Hesburgh himself pointed out that, in 1967, Notre Dame was a vastly different institution from the school Father Edward Sorin, CSC, founded in 1842. It had grown from three log cabins to "more than one hundred substantial buildings, a radio and TV station, fire and police departments, a massive food service operation, a highly competitive varsity athletics program, a bookstore, a hotel, seven thousand acres of property in Wisconsin, academic facilities in London, Rome, and Jerusalem, and a program for the future that would require us to raise, invest, and spend hundreds of millions of dollars each and every year."[11] Notre Dame was far too complex an undertaking to be run like a mom and pop store.

The larger context of higher education had also changed dramatically—especially over the first fifteen years that Hesburgh served as president. The arrival of the baby boomers transformed American colleges and universities. Not only did they launch the era of student protest and campus unrest that we know as "the sixties," but also their sheer numbers led to more mundane changes: expanding facilities, increased spending, and bulging administration. A new level of complexity entered into managing universities, sparking a movement among state schools to professionalize their boards of trustees.

Catholic universities faced similar pressures. They also began to worry about being left behind. Catholic educators received a shock in 1966 when the Court of Appeals in Maryland ruled in the *Horace Mann* case that two Catholic colleges were ineligible for state grants on the grounds that they were "sectarian" and thus barred from state support by the establishment clause of the US Constitution. The ruling sent a chill down the spine of Catholic college presidents across the country, who desperately needed state and federal funding to survive. It gave urgency to the question of the precise relationship between the universities and the church.

A series of highly publicized controversies in the mid-1960s over academic freedom at Catholic universities further complicated matters. In 1963, the rector of The Catholic University of America barred four progressive theologians from speaking on campus, sparking widespread protest in both the Catholic and secular press.[12] That same year, the Congregation for Seminaries and Universities quietly issued a decree that all honorary degrees awarded by Catholic universities had to be approved by the Vatican, which prompted an impassioned defense of institutional autonomy by none other than Cardinal Spellman of New York. In December 1965, Saint John's University in New York abruptly fired thirty-one professors (clerical and lay) in the name of preserving the institution's basic religious character—a violation of academic due process that set off a faculty strike. Shortly after, a philosophy professor at the University of Dayton charged members of his department with heresy, drawing an initially reluctant Archbishop Karl Alter into the fray. And at Catholic University, academic life ground to a halt in 1967 when faculty and students united to protest the board of trustees' decision to terminate the appointment of the widely respected moral theologian Father Charles Curran.[13]

Hesburgh was keenly aware of these developments. He also knew what he wanted, and he knew that getting there would take a lot of money. In urging his Holy Cross brothers to transfer governance to a lay board, Hesburgh cited the Maryland case, which threatened government grants, and he alluded to the recent controversies over academic freedom, which made private foundations wary. A large and robust board of trustees would also be a potential source of donations.[14] Hesburgh wanted the university to do great things and he felt hemmed in by outdated structures. Years later, he quipped: "I knew that if I were going to see Notre Dame grow into a first-rate Catholic University I could no longer have to get permission from a Provincial every time I needed a new lawn mower!"[15]

Hesburgh seems to have first raised the governance issue in the spring of 1965. He was in Chicago visiting the home of Edmund Stephan, an attorney and alum who served on Notre Dame's Advisory Board of Lay Trustees. The board had been created in 1921 to advise university leadership on investments and other financial matters. Hesburgh valued the board's professional expertise and often used the group as an informal sounding board. He counted Stephan a close friend. Stephan remembered lying in bed, recovering from surgery, chatting with Hesburgh for two or three hours. Hesburgh was talking about all the changes in the church and the world, how they were all coming so quickly, and how "the effects of Vatican II were sweeping through the church." The emerging role of the laity, Hesburgh told Stephan, "was something we all had to face up to if the church was to remain vital."[16] He talked about changing the governance structure at Notre Dame and asked Stephan to explore the legal ramifications of such a move.

In June of 1966, Hesburgh and Stephan met at the Land O'Lakes retreat with a small group that included the Holy Cross Superior General, Father Germain Lalande, the Provincial, Father Howard ("Doc") Kenna, the university vice presidents, and several key lay advisors. They agreed to move forward according to a plan laid out by Stephan.

Further meetings were held that fall. In January, a special chapter meeting of the Holy Cross province approved the change by a vote of thirty-eight to four. The Superior General endorsed it, and the Vatican gave permission. By May, Hesburgh could assemble reporters in his newly constructed Center for Continuing Education and announce that the deal was done.

In his memoir, Hesburgh characterized the change as a decision to "give away" the university "lock, stock, and barrel."[17] In reality, it was less a transfer of property *from* Holy Cross *to* lay leaders, and more an expansion of governance to include laypeople formally in the decision making of the university. Hesburgh saw in the new arrangement an opportunity to model for the rest of the church the kind of partnership envisioned by the Second Vatican Council. The Notre Dame community was in a unique position to give leadership to other institutions, to show "that Catholicism and freedom are not incompatible and priests and laymen can work together."[18] As soon as the new board of trustees was constituted, it confirmed Father Hesburgh as university president and elected Ed Stephan its first lay chair.

The change in governance proceeded smoothly; and within a few years, the vast majority of Catholic colleges and universities in the United States followed suit. At the same time, the change raised new questions about what it means to be a university that is truly Catholic. When schools were owned and operated by priests and nuns, when students and faculty were all Catholic, when Mass attendance was recorded and catechetical classes required, Catholic identity was largely taken for granted. At places like Notre Dame, this presumption of Catholicity still held in 1967. During debates at the provincial chapter over transferring governance, a few priests raised concerns about secularization, but they were quickly dismissed. The questions voiced were more about the prerogatives of the Holy Cross community than they were about the underlying Catholic character of the institution. At the press conference announcing the new board arrangement, Hesburgh assured his listeners that the most important responsibility of the Board of Fellows was to maintain "the essential character of the university as a Catholic institution of higher learning."[19] But what would that mean?

Hesburgh had been asking that question ever since John Cavanaugh handed him the key to the president's office. He knew that any answer would have to reconcile the normative faith claims of the Catholic Church with the spirit of open inquiry that defined the academic enterprise. It would have to affirm both religious commitment and academic freedom, both faith and reason. It would also have to confront an unfortunate history of excessive control and censorship by the church's hierarchy.

In 1963, Hesburgh had been elected president of the International Federation of Catholic Universities (IFCU)—a moribund organization that its members hoped he would revitalize. Hesburgh reluctantly agreed and, shortly thereafter, was summoned to Rome for what he thought would be a swearing-in ceremony. Instead, he was called on the carpet by the cardinal head of the Sacred Congregation of Seminaries and Universities, to be informed that his election was invalid. Hesburgh could not be the president of the Federation, Cardinal Pizzardo said, because he was not the president of a Catholic university. Apparently, those who had lost out in the election had used their influence with the cardinal to conjure up an excuse based on the fact that Notre Dame (like virtually every other Catholic university in the United States) had never requested an official pontifical charter.

"That's a laugh," Hesburgh recalled saying. "We've been a member of the Federation as a Catholic university since its inception and no one ever returned our annual dues." When the cardinal got up to leave, Hesburgh demanded that he be heard out. "I told him that we would not stand for his autocratic plan and neither would the people who had elected us, and if he persisted he would just end up being in charge of nothing." According to Hesburgh, "I really let the fur fly."[20]

The incident clearly touched a nerve. No doubt it brought to mind an earlier run-in with the Vatican that took place in Hesburgh's second year as university president. In 1954, Cardinal Alfredo Ottaviani—the powerful head of the Holy Office, who would go on to lead the conservative resistance at Vatican II—demanded that Notre Dame withdraw a volume of conference proceedings that featured an article by the American Jesuit Father John Courtney Murray. At the time Murray was under suspicion in Rome for his progressive views on religious freedom. Ottaviani wanted to silence Murray, and so he ordered the Holy Cross Superior General, Father Christopher O'Toole, to put pressure on Hesburgh to comply.

The directive, Hesburgh remembered, "hit me like a challenge to action." The very existence of the university seemed on the line. "There was no way I was going to destroy the freedom and autonomy of the university and, indeed, the university itself, when so many people had devoted their lives to building it. . . . Notre Dame would lose all its credibility in the United States, and so would I, if an official in Rome could abrogate our academic freedom with a snap of his fingers."[21] Hesburgh threatened to resign rather than compromise the academic integrity of the university. He refused to suppress the volume and later proposed a face-saving alternative.

The impasse over his election to lead the IFCU was only finally resolved when Hesburgh asked Pope Paul VI to intervene. But the incident remained for Hesburgh a cautionary tale about the danger of Vatican interference in the internal workings of academic institutions. At the IFCU's 1965 meeting in Tokyo, the first under Hesburgh's leadership, the Federation took up the question of institutional autonomy directly and then turned to a more fundamental set of issues. Inspired by Vatican II's call for renewal, the organization would focus its next international conference (to take place in 1968 in Kinshasa) on the question: What is the nature and role of the Catholic university in the modern world? It was the question to which Hesburgh had dedicated his life.

In preparation for Kinshasa, seminars were to be held in each of the four regions of the IFCU. The North American group—led by Hesburgh himself—decided to meet at Notre Dame's Land O'Lakes property in order to draft their position paper. In July 1967, just two months after Notre Dame introduced its new lay board of trustees, twenty-six men came together at the Wisconsin retreat. It included Hesburgh and Ed Stephan, Superior General Lalande and "Doc" Kenna. Father Paul Reinert, SJ, the president of Saint Louis University, was also there; and he brought along the chair of SLU's own newly constituted lay board, Daniel Schlafly. Several other university presidents and administrators, the Assistant General of the Jesuits, two bishops (including the chair of the US bishops' committee on higher education), and the journalist John Cogley rounded out the group. No women were invited—a gross oversight given the large network of colleges run by sisters and nuns.[22]

The gathering gained a notoriety that few of its participants anticipated. The short statement they produced quickly "took on a life of its own as a symbolic manifesto," the herald of a new era in Catholic higher education.[23] Its very first lines challenged Catholic institutions to become universities "in the full modern sense of the word" with a driving commitment to academic excellence. To achieve its ends, the statement continued, the Catholic university "must have a true autonomy and academic freedom in the face of authority of whatever kind, lay or clerical, external to the academic community itself."[24] Wrapped up in the revolutionary moment that was the summer of 1967, these words were in their own way a revolution. For many Catholic educators, emboldened by postconciliar changes and new university governing structures, the document's opening salvo rang like a "declaration of independence" from the church and its hierarchy.[25]

Despite these opening lines—and in contrast to the turmoil of the times—the rest of the "Land O'Lakes Statement" was relatively serene. The statement's emphasis on autonomy was uncompromising and unapologetic. At the same time, the bulk of the text stressed how Catholicism is to be "perceptively present and effectively operative" in the life of the university.[26] The text was drafted by SLU's academic vice president, Father Robert Henle, SJ, but the ideas were all Hesburgh. His commitment to academic excellence, his confidence in the power of dialogue, and his unfailing Christian optimism permeate the document. Consistent with Hesburgh's vision, the academic study of theology holds pride of place. For a university to be Catholic, theology must not only be recognized as a legitimate discipline, it must also be seen as "essential to the integrity" of the university itself. However, unlike an earlier era, theology can no longer serve as an integrating force: "There must be no theological or philosophical imperialism." Each of the university disciplines enjoys its own internal autonomy and its own distinctive approaches and methodologies, which need to be respected. Rather than synthesis or integration, the statement recommended dialogue—"interdisciplinary discussion"—that moves in two directions. First, theologians must confront "all the rest of modern culture and all the areas of intellectual study which it includes." Second, scholars in other disciplines need to be open to recognizing that "there is a philosophical and theological dimension to most intellectual subjects when they are pursued far enough."[27]

The gathering at Land O'Lakes helped to solidify what could be considered Hesburgh's mature vision of the Catholic university, a vision that he articulated with particular force on December 9, 1967, at a convocation marking Notre Dame's 125th anniversary. He later described this speech as "the most important talk I have ever written," and he returned to its themes for the rest of his career.[28] Echoing the Land O'Lakes Statement, Hesburgh asserted that a Catholic university "must first and foremost be a university."[29] To be a university is to be a place "where all the relevant questions are asked and where answers are elaborated in an atmosphere of freedom and responsible inquiry." Thus a university cannot and should not be ruled by any authority external to the university itself. "The best and only traditional authority in the university is intellectual competence: this is the coin of the realm."[30]

A great Catholic university must be a great university, but it must be something more. For Hesburgh, *catholic* means universal, and a *Catholic* university implies a universality of knowledge. Returning to themes he had sounded for years, Hesburgh argued that such a universality of knowledge demands the presence of philosophy and theology in the university. Theology, in particular, must be engaged "on the highest level of intellectual inquiry" so that it can be "in living dialogue with all the other disciplines in the university."[31] This dialogue is a two-way street, which Hesburgh captured in the phrase: *intellectus quaerens fidem et fides quaerens intellectum* ("understanding seeking faith and faith seeking understanding").[32] On the one hand, Saint Anselm of Canterbury's classic definition of theology as "faith seeking understanding" calls the theologian, rooted in faith, to seek understanding in every disciplinary corner the modern university provides. On the other hand, the scientist, the engineer, the poet, and all those living the intellectual life seek "faith"—that is, they seek "a deeper meaning" running through their pursuits.

In fostering this dialogue, the university—like the priest—serves as a mediator. The Catholic university can do what others cannot: "give living witness to the wholeness of truth from all sources, both human and divine, while recognizing the inner sacredness of all truth from whatever source, and the validity and autonomy of all paths to truth."[33] However, to serve as mediator does not mean that the Catholic university functions as a value-free arbiter. "The mediator stands in the middle, but he stands for something, else he is a mighty poor mediator." What does the Catholic university stand for? Here Hesburgh is unambiguous: "We know that God has spoken to man and we think this important enough to be reckoned with in all else we know, or believe we know, from whatever source."[34] To stand "between" the realm of human knowledge and the saving message of Christ is to make a claim for the transcendent.

Hesburgh concluded his 1967 address with a troika of metaphors that he would repeat for the rest of his life. They provide concrete images illustrating different aspects of the abstract notion of mediation that was so central to Hesburgh's own sense of mission. A great Catholic university is a *beacon* shining with the light of its commitment to reason illuminated by faith. It is a *bridge* stretching across the many chasms that separate people, disciplines, and ideas from one another. Finally, it is a *crossroads* where all the intellectual and moral currents of the contemporary world meet.

The bold confidence of the Land O'Lakes Statement was much more a product of the optimistic years leading up to 1967 than it was a portent of the pessimism to come. Hesburgh's own hopefulness and idealism never lagged, but he soon faced—on multiple fronts—the real difficulty of building bridges in a world where "everything became unhinged at once."[35]

The first stirrings of student unrest surfaced long before Land O'Lakes, and they revolved around what today might seem like trivial matters concerning campus rules and regulations. In 1960, Notre Dame was still governed by the *in loco parentis* system, in which the university saw itself as the parental authority over students while they lived on campus. Mass was required three mornings a week; the curfew was midnight (lights out at 1 a.m. on weekends); there was no underage drinking, no cars on campus, and absolutely no female visitors in dorm rooms.

Although Hesburgh's goal was to modernize the university, he drew a line when it came to student behavior. Progressive on civil rights, he was decidedly conservative on the relationship between the sexes. When local media publicized a Notre Dame "panty raid" at nearby Saint Mary's College, he was mortified. "Hesburgh was so angry that I thought he was going to explode," said one colleague.[36]

Hesburgh supported the *in loco parentis* system because he believed that the university had a responsibility to form not only students' intellect but also their character. However, he gradually came to see that adjustments could be made without abandoning that goal. In response to intense pressure, he allowed modest changes to the rules in 1961 and approved a revised student manual, "rewritten to convey a more positive attitude toward student behavior."[37] Students were not satisfied. They continued to complain about the paternalistic regulations governing life on campus. Frustration came to a head in the spring of 1963. In response to strident demands for change, the administration censored three articles in the student magazine *The Scholastic*. "The student romance with Fr. Hesburgh is over," the magazine editorialized, and then called on Hesburgh to step down as president.[38] Since he was away from campus so often, the editorial continued, he should take up a new position as chancellor and turn over the day-to-day operation of the university to a lay president. Shortly thereafter, student leaders drafted a "Declaration of Student Rights and Grievances," challenging the role of the Holy Cross order in overseeing student life and demanding an end to the *in loco parentis* system.[39]

Hesburgh responded with a scathing letter sent to every student at their parents' address. He fiercely defended the dedication of his fellow Holy Cross priests and his own leadership of the university. He acknowledged that "the Winter of our discontent" at Notre Dame was part of a larger spiritual malaise, a larger impulse on the part of youth to challenge authority, which certainly had its place. However, Hesburgh would not tolerate irresponsible or ill-informed criticism, nor would he abandon what he believed best for the community. Notre Dame did not consider "students to be equal partners in the educative process." Those who can't live by the rules should get free from Notre Dame, not "expect Notre Dame to lose its unique character." The primary responsibility of students "is to learn and not to teach," Hesburgh bristled. "Students who think otherwise should go out and found their own universities and then take lessons from their students."[40]

The letter was probably the low point in Hesburgh's relationship with students. One of the things that bothered him most was that young people got so worked up about the "petty concerns" of campus life while seeming to ignore the many pressing challenges facing the nation and the world.[41] That, of course, was about to change.

In the fall of 1964, students at the University of California at Berkeley came together under the banner of the Free Speech Movement to launch an unprecedented series of student strikes and mass rallies. A thousand students occupied the university's Sproul Hall only to be forcibly removed by police, sparking further demonstrations.

The student revolution had begun. What started out as a local issue—a protest against campus policy banning certain political activities—quickly took on broader significance. The unrest spread to campuses around the country, and the concerns expanded from academic freedom to issues of race, gender, civil liberties, corporate complicity, and, above all, the war being waged in Vietnam.

Things remained relatively calm at Notre Dame, particularly compared to the violence erupting elsewhere. In May 1966, twenty-five students picketed the annual ROTC review. The following year, the number had risen to 350. Still, as late as October 1967, Hesburgh could confidently proclaim that Notre Dame was having no serious problems with drugs, hippies, or protestors—"just a few beards and I have nothing against beards."[42]

However, the student uprising at Columbia the following April put every college president in the country on notice. The radical group Students for a Democratic Society broke into the office of Columbia's president, Grayson Kirk. They barricaded themselves inside, ransacked his files, smoked his cigars, and defecated on his rug. In the midst of the Columbia protests came the devastating news that Martin Luther King, Jr., had been assassinated. That summer, Bobby Kennedy was killed. The Tet Offensive intensified anti-war anger and paralyzed the Johnson administration. The Democratic National Convention descended into chaos. Student revolts exploded across Europe. "As one who lived through that whole period," Hesburgh reflected, "I would like to assure one and all that it was a most unpleasant experience. . . . The unheard of and unprecedented happened daily. Nothing seemed right and everything wrong. Moreover, almost nothing one tried worked, and one had the feeling in the pit of one's stomach of being perpetually the small boy with his finger in the dike, holding back the flood, precariously."[43]

Hesburgh knew Columbia's Kirk well, as he did many other college presidents subjected to violent demonstrations and other "outrages."[44] During those years, Hesburgh carried a sheet of yellow legal paper in his coat pocket on which he kept a handwritten list of all the major university presidents who had been driven out of office by the student rebellion. Perhaps he feared that his own name would soon be added to it. According to his biographer Michael O'Brien, student activists at Notre Dame had a "love-hate" relationship with their famous president. They knew that Father Hesburgh had transformed the university in beneficial ways, and that he was a reasonable dialogue partner. They were well aware of his work for civil rights, but, as one student leader recalled, "we never perceived Fr. Hesburgh as liberal or as civil libertarian as he was perceived . . . outside the university." Activist students thought of him as the "Great Establishmentarian."[45]

The increasing—and increasingly intense—confrontations with students began to wear on Hesburgh. Black students on campus challenged his civil rights bona fides by pointing out the lack of diversity on campus. At a Notre Dame conference on racism, students baited their president. One black student dismissed his record as hypocritical: "The Civil Rights Commission was created by The Man to study black people. Well, let me tell *you* something, Father Hesburgh; we've been studied enough! What we want now are deeds, and if you're committed to the cause of black people, then why don't you show it here at Notre Dame?"[46]

At the Georgia Tech game in November 1968, over forty student members of the Afro-American Society marched through Notre Dame Stadium with signs that read "Ara, the day of the lily-white backfields is past" and "Hesburgh of the Civil Rights Commission: Check on your own backyard." They were met with racial slurs ("Get off the field you dirty niggers!" and "White Power forever!") shouted from the overwhelmingly white student section—a reaction that disturbed Hesburgh more than the protest itself.[47]

Monday after the game, a previously scheduled three-day demonstration began on the second floor of Notre Dame's Main Building. As many as three hundred students gathered to protest the presence on campus of recruiters from the CIA and Dow Chemical (which produced the napalm used in Vietnam). The demonstration culminated on Wednesday when fifty students staged a four-hour "lie-in" that blocked the door of the placement office where interviews were to be held.

In the midst of unrest, Hesburgh tried to chart a middle course—upholding the right of students to protest but demanding that they also respect the rights of others. By blocking the door with their bodies, Hesburgh concluded, demonstrators had crossed the line and "used their freedom of action to obstruct the freedom of others and impose their own personal convictions on others."[48] In an open letter, Hesburgh asked the entire Notre Dame community to help decide how it was going to respond in the future. "I could have acted unilaterally, and many have accused me of weakness or lack of leadership in not doing so. However, I much prefer to appeal to you, for this is your community and your University and it cannot be what it should be without your support."[49]

After further incidents on campus—including a conference on pornography that ended with local police confiscating an unauthorized film and then spraying mace at students in order to escape the angry crowd—Hesburgh decided to act. He consulted faculty, student, and alumni groups before issuing a policy, which he explained in an eight-page letter, addressed "Dear Notre Dame Faculty and Students" and dated February 17, 1969.

In the letter, Hesburgh acknowledged that there was plenty going wrong in the world to justify protest. The question was how to proceed. "The last thing a shaken society needs is more shaking. The last think a noisy, turbulent, and disintegrating community needs is more noise, turbulence, and disintegration." The university has a unique role to play in addressing the ills of society "by bringing all its intellectual and moral powers to bear upon them."[50] The university cannot do everything, Hesburgh argued, but it was still "one of man's best hopes in these troubled times." And so he recommitted Notre Dame to be "ready and prepared and anxious to respond to every intellectual and moral concern in the world today, in every way proper to the university. . . . We only insist on the rights of all, minority and majority, the climate of civility and rationality, and a preponderant moral abhorrence of violence or inhuman forms of persuasion that violate our style of life and the nature of the university."[51]

On the specific issue of how the university would respond to demonstrators who violated the rights of others or impeded the normal life of the community, Hesburgh was firm:

> May I begin by saying that all of this is hypothetical and I personally hope it never happens here at Notre Dame. But, if it does, anyone or any group that substitutes force for rational persuasion, be it violent or nonviolent, will be given fifteen minutes of meditation to cease and desist. . . . If they do not within that time period cease and desist, they will be asked for their identity cards. Those who produce these will be suspended from this community as not understanding what this community is. Those who do not have or will not produce identity cards will be assumed not to be members of the community and will be charged with trespassing and disturbing the peace on private property and treated accordingly by the law.[52]

The response to the letter was overwhelming. "Perhaps it was merely the right tone of letter at the right time," he reflected. "It was the first of its kind from a university president, the first firm drawing of the line on student protests, and it was widely taken as a blueprint of sorts for other colleges and universities."[53] Clearly, Hesburgh struck a chord. Within a few days, some two hundred fifty newspapers had covered the letter, almost all praising Hesburgh's tough stand. Both *The New York Times* and *The Wall Street Journal* carried the full text. Notre Dame's press office was inundated with requests for interviews. A photograph at the time shows Hesburgh's secretary, Helen Hosinski, buried under an avalanche of letters sent in support.

As would be expected, students criticized the fifteen-minute rule. The former editor of the *Observer*, Robert Sam Anson, then working for *Time* magazine, sent Hesburgh a telegram "sadly but strongly" suggesting he resign.[54] Others dismissed the approach as unrealistic. Such strong-arm tactics might work with compliant Notre Dame students, but on any other campus, they would burn the place down. Senator Eugene McCarthy joked that such a policy at such a place was a bit like warning an all-girl band not to chew tobacco. The first and only time Hesburgh's fifteen-minute rule went into effect was that fall, when ten Notre Dame students, again attempting to block interviews with the CIA and Dow, were suspended for refusing to comply with university policy. All but one later returned to Notre Dame to complete their degrees.[55]

Hesburgh complained that the press focused too much on what the letter said about expulsion but hardly ever mentioned what it said about the legitimacy of protest. He saw the statement as an attempt to correct a balance that had been lost by administrators who turned their universities over to student radicals.

Hardliners saw the statement as a gift from heaven. "I came off sounding like a superhawk, which I was not," Hesburgh lamented.[56] When President Nixon sent a four-page telegram congratulating him for his tough stand on student violence, Hesburgh grew concerned. He knew the administration wanted to advance restrictive legislation to clamp down on student protests. Nixon asked Hesburgh to advise Vice President Agnew, who was meeting with the governors of all fifty states in order to pitch the idea. Hesburgh responded with a hastily written, but eloquent, letter insisting that "universities and colleges should handle their own problems, make their own decisions, without the intervention of the federal government except upon invitation."[57] The letter arrived in the middle of the meeting and proved decisive in turning the tide away from any repressive legislation.

Perhaps because he had become identified with a hardline stance, Hesburgh increasingly felt the need to defend the students and the legitimacy of their protests. Many years later, Hesburgh wrote: "Through it all, I never thought the student revolution was all that bad. . . . These young people were demonstrating their enormous energy, commitment, and dedication to ideals with which few of us could argue." As children, these young adults were taught to believe in the American dream. "And then they grew up and suddenly came upon the realization that this nation was not one and indivisible. It was clearly divided between the whites and the blacks, the affluent and the poor, the hopeful and the hopeless. They saw inequalities all around them which contradicted what the 'older generation' was telling them in and out of our universities."[58] Even in the midst of the strife, Hesburgh defended the students' concerns—despite all the headaches they caused. When a reporter, with an air of superiority, asked why he wasted his time with these rebellious kids, Hesburgh shot back, "What is so good about you or your world?" He asked: "Is there nothing to be uneasy about, nothing to protest, nothing to revolt against? . . . We might begin by trying to understand what causes the unrest, the protest, the revolt of the young people today."[59]

During World War II, Hesburgh dreamed of serving as a Navy chaplain in the Pacific. He was an ardent supporter of ROTC at Notre Dame. His patriotism was sincere and his belief in the moral purpose of America was real. At first, Hesburgh judged the Vietnam conflict as merely the latest effort—tragic, but necessary—by the United States to fight the forces of evil and injustice in the world. Up until 1968, he believed the use of force in Vietnam was morally permissible. That began to change, as the futility of the war led Hesburgh to reconsider his position. More importantly, the conviction and passion of the student protestors challenged Hesburgh. "They gave him his conscience," said a colleague.[60] "The old 'God, Country and Notre Dame' patriotism had been in place in the mid-1960s," explained Thomas Shaffer, dean of the law school at the time. "Then you had a period of that patriotic resolve gradually eroding. After 1970, Notre Dame was, by and large, a place of protest against the war, heavily because of Father Hesburgh's leadership—but he, too, had changed his mind."[61]

On October 14, 1969, Hesburgh announced that he had added his name to a letter signed by several prominent college presidents calling for the withdrawal of US forces from Vietnam. The next day, he joined 2,500 students in front of the library for a peace Mass. "Conspicuous in his presence," Hesburgh watched as four students and two professors tore apart their draft cards at the offertory.[62] He began to speak out more forcefully on Vietnam, favoring a cease fire and internationally supervised elections. By the following spring, when President Nixon went on television to defend sending troops into Cambodia, Hesburgh was firmly opposed to US involvement in Vietnam.

Nixon's address to the nation on April 30, 1970, unleashed a fury of student protests that was unprecedented in scope and intensity—even by the standards of the turbulent 1960s. In the days that followed, 100,000 demonstrators descended on Washington, and hundreds of thousands of students nationwide went on strike, shutting down more than 450 schools. As many as thirty ROTC buildings were set ablaze. And, on May 4, National Guardsmen trying to disperse a demonstration at Kent State University shot and killed four students, injuring ten others.

The day after Nixon's speech, a group of thirty to forty Notre Dame students invaded the Center for Continuing

Education, disrupting the Board of Trustees' end-of-year meeting. The following Monday, a huge rally was planned on campus. Hesburgh spent the weekend dealing with one confrontation after another, returning to his office Sunday night exhausted. Shortly after midnight, a student knocked on his door to warn him that one of the groups was planning to burn down the ROTC building the next day. Around two o'clock in the morning, another student came to inform Hesburgh that he should expect an invitation to speak at the Monday rally, but should know that it was a ploy to set him up for some kind of embarrassment. Knowing what he was getting himself into, Hesburgh began to write out carefully what he wanted to say. When the head of student government, Dave Krashna, called around three o'clock to invite Hesburgh to speak, he agreed. Hesburgh finished his remarks around four thirty, left the text for Helen Hosinski to type when she got in, and went to bed.[63]

The following afternoon, before a crowd of two thousand students and faculty, Hesburgh condemned the war in Vietnam unequivocally. But he challenged students to find a more constructive response than a strike. "Striking classes as some universities are doing, in the sense of cutting off your education, is the worst thing you could do at this time, since your education and your growth in competence are what the world needs most, if the leadership of the future is going to be better than the leadership of the past and present." Departing from his text, Hesburgh said, "We are living in an age of midgets, I want you to prepare to be giants."[64]

As he spoke, news of the Kent State shootings spread through the crowd. Yet, Hesburgh was able to channel the anger and frustration of students in a way few leaders at the time could. He concluded with a six-point "declaration," which called for: immediate withdrawal of troops; repatriation of American prisoners of war; rebuilding Vietnamese society; support for self-governance; a commitment to human, rather than military, priorities; and a promise "to commit our persons, our talents, our honor, and our futures to help work for a better America and a better world in a peaceful and non-violent manner."[65] Hesburgh said he would be proud to sign this statement alongside students and convey it to President Nixon.

After Hesburgh left the stage, Krashna ignored his counsel and called for a strike. A number of students, however, had begun to imagine different ways of responding. When Hesburgh got back to his office, he found a group of students waiting outside the door. They wanted copies of his speech, which they planned to take to every household in South Bend to gather signatures. A spontaneous canvassing effort took off. Within a few days, as many as one thousand students had gone door-to-door, collecting 23,000 signatures in support of the six-point "Hesburgh Declaration," which its author proudly sent on to President Nixon, as promised.

Classes were eventually suspended that week, replaced with "teach-ins," student-organized demonstrations, and a letter-writing campaign. On Wednesday, five thousand people marched peacefully from the Notre Dame campus to a rally at South Bend's Howard Park. The next day, Ascension Thursday, Hesburgh eulogized the slain Kent State students and called for a nation in which "ballots replaced bullets." By Monday, May 11, campus was beginning to return to normal. When Hesburgh took the stage that night to introduce a speech by the anti-war senator from Indiana, Vance Hartke, students gave Father Ted a one-minute standing ovation.

Over the course of seven days, the university had moved from the brink of chaos and division to a spirit of solidarity and common purpose. Even those who disagreed with his anti-war stance admired the way Hesburgh had "a personally stabilizing effect on the university in that week."[66]

Hesburgh was one of the few prominent college presidents who survived the upheaval of the student protests. When asked if he ever regretted taking on the job as president, he smiled: "About ten times a week." One of his standard jokes at the time told the story of a university president who died and went to hell: It was four days before he noticed the difference. According to Michael O'Brien, Hesburgh managed the crisis by staying connected, maintaining contact with all his constituencies, and winning their respect.[67] He genuinely served as a bridge builder, insisting that opposing camps meet one another in a spirit of dialogue, civility, and respect for the rights of others. In the end, he believed that all the upheaval of the student revolution was a good thing. Universities emerged chastened, but wiser and stronger. Less than five years after that tumultuous week in the spring of 1970, Hesburgh reflected:

> While the sixties were difficult for everyone in the university, they were not in vain. One should not exaggerate either the good or the bad results of the student revolution, but on some presently quiet evenings—when the library fills up as students study and seek security for the future and are not greatly concerned, as they once were, about festering world problems—one might ask whether it would not be helpful to have a touch of continuing revolution in the educational process. We have learned that universities can certainly be too noisy. But they can also be too quiet.[68]

CHAPTER SIX

The Humane Imperative

Hesburgh weathered the storm of the sixties and emerged on the other side with his reputation not only intact, but undeniably enhanced. His many external engagements cemented the image of the Holy Cross priest as a strong moral voice willing to address the most important challenges of the day. He was rightly recognized as a champion of civil rights, a proponent of peaceful exchange between the nuclear powers, an untiring advocate for human rights, a staunch defender of academic freedom, and an inspiring model of Vatican II's call for a faith actively engaged in the world.

On campus, Hesburgh successfully navigated through any number of shoals on which the university could have easily run aground. He established institutional autonomy without abandoning Notre Dame's Catholic identity. He relaxed rules in the residence halls while insisting on the administration's role in the moral formation of students. He condemned the war in Vietnam while commending those who served in that war. He responded to campus demonstrations firmly and decisively, at the same time displaying genuine sympathy for the very real concerns of students. All in all, it was an impressive bit of sailing. And it did not go unnoticed. In 1972 two former students, Joel Connelly and Howard Dooley, published a book-length chronicle of this turbulent time. Adopting a narrative of achievement that had already taken hold, they titled their story *Hesburgh's Notre Dame: Triumph in Transition*.

If Hesburgh had been triumphant, he certainly didn't rest on his laurels. He quickly pivoted from past accomplishment to future work. In 1973 Hesburgh delivered the prestigious Terry Lectures at Yale University, later published as *The Humane Imperative: A Challenge for the Year 2000*. Declaring himself a "Christian optimist" without apology, Hesburgh began these lectures with his deep conviction that "we can affect the course of our times." Insofar as theological and philosophical principles become operative in all of our social, economic, political, and scientific activities, "the world will become better, more human, even somewhat divine and—in the incarnational sense of the English word—godly."[1]

His hope-filled reflections on interfaith cooperation, human dignity, the green revolution, and international development reflect Hesburgh's growing attention to issues of global concern. For a decade and a half, Hesburgh had thrown himself into what he considered the most difficult domestic challenge facing the nation, civil rights. From the 1970s forward, he would direct his energies toward those challenges looming over the whole world—poverty and hunger, war and peace, human rights and the ecological crisis. With the American bicentennial on the horizon, Hesburgh proposed his own Declaration of *Interdependence* of all humankind. For Hesburgh, only a bold vision of the equality, the oneness, and the dignity of all people could make possible a future of peace and promise aboard "Spaceship Earth."[2]

In 1971 Hesburgh agreed to serve as chair of the Overseas Development Council (ODC), a private, nonprofit foundation established two years earlier to draw attention to the needs of underdeveloped countries. He quickly became a leading advocate for international humanitarian aid. When crop failures sparked mass starvation in Bangladesh, Hesburgh lobbied President Ford to take action. In an open letter on November 22, 1974, he called on the president to increase US food aid. The two men exchanged several letters, and Hesburgh kept up the pressure. He went on the *Today Show* to draw attention to the issue. When he was asked why Americans should help these poor countries, Hesburgh responded simply, "[We] ought to do it because it's the right thing to do. It's being human; it's being Christian. . . . [It's] doing the kind of thing that human beings ought to do, being compassionate toward each other."[3] Hesburgh's efforts made a difference. When President Ford spoke at Notre Dame the following spring, he told faculty and students that Hesburgh's advocacy was an important factor in his decision to send more aid abroad.

For Hesburgh the world food crisis was the "moral imperative of our day." The "energy crisis" that so preoccupied Americans in the mid-1970s was a mere inconvenience when compared to the catastrophe of widespread starvation. "If you run out of gas," he told one audience, "you can't go on a picnic in the country but if you run out of food, you die."[4] Hesburgh argued that the commitment of so many Americans to confront racial prejudice must be matched by an equal passion to redress *geographic* prejudice—the huge disparities between people based simply on where they were born. "We in the northern part of this globe worry about overproducing Ph.D.'s; many children in the Southern Hemisphere never enter a school. We speak of heart and kidney transplants; they never see a doctor from birth to death. . . . We are often overfed and overweight; they are undernourished from birth, often suffering brain damage therefrom. We speak often of second homes; they live in cardboard or mud and wattle huts."[5] The wealthy nations are responsible for creating "a world of incredible global discontinuities and injustices," and thus have a responsibility to respond.

The problems of the world did not paralyze Hesburgh but prompted him to take action. "One gets the feeling," wrote a reporter for the *Chicago Tribune*, that "he would grab his perpetually packed satchel and head for the door if he suspected some mover and shaker would implement the plan he has."[6] Hesburgh was an idealist who believed practical solutions were possible. He marveled at scientific advances in agriculture and communications technology, opening up new vistas for crop cultivation and education. Rather than look at the difficulties as insurmountable, Hesburgh said, "I would prefer to look at the new opportunities and creative responses" that are within reach. "Human ingenuity in the face of crisis," he believed, was one of humankind's "greatest glories."[7] In the face of widespread famine, Hesburgh could understand why so many well-intentioned people were overwhelmed, pessimistic, or discouraged. "Yet, I am not a prophet of gloom and doom," he proclaimed. "It will get better," Hesburgh believed, "but only if we can change profoundly, only if interdependence passes from an idea to a fruitful and operative reality in the political, economic, and social life of the whole planet."[8]

Hesburgh's extensive travels brought him face to face with the suffering of the poor in the developing world, instilling in him a genuine concern for their plight. He saw up close the terrible effects of famine and hunger. "There are few sights more heart rending than human beings without food or drink," Hesburgh reflected. "One understands, in seeing them, the premium the good Lord placed on feeding the hungry and giving drink to the thirsty."[9] No doubt these experiences abroad fueled Hesburgh's passion for helping those suffering in the developing world. But his perspective on the global food crisis was also shaped by conversations closer to home. Through his work with the Rockefeller Foundation, Hesburgh was drawn into larger philanthropic efforts to address the issues of disease, hunger, and poverty in the developing world.

In 1961, John D. Rockefeller III, the grandson of the oil tycoon, invited Hesburgh to join the board of the Rockefeller Foundation. At the time, Rockefeller headed up a small but influential group of government and industry leaders in the United States who had become convinced that a global hunger crisis was looming. Reviving the predictions of the nineteenth-century philosopher Thomas Malthus, they argued that the geometric rate of population growth would eventually outpace food production, with dire results. "The Second World War proved all too clearly the consequences of what happens when nations experience food and natural resource shortages and the lack of living space to support their populations." Overpopulation, advocates argued, led to political, social, and economic instability. A shared sentiment started to take hold: "To make the world safe for American democracy, global population needed to be controlled. American know-how and technology were needed to avert another war."[10]

Through their well-funded lobbying efforts, population advocates raised public awareness and advanced public policy. Thus the 1960s became a decade of "population anxiety." Articles appeared in parenting magazines. Major news outlets covered the story. A line warning of the "race between food supply and population" made its way into President Lyndon Johnson's State of the Union address. "Family planning" entered into federal legislation and soon became an essential component of social welfare programs. In this, the United States was not alone, as concerns about overpopulation spread across Europe and Asia. Even the Vatican was drawn into this global conversation. The urgency of the issue was captured at a popular level by Paul Ehrlich, who, in his best-selling book *The Population Bomb*, predicted that the 1970s would be a decade of mass starvation, environmental catastrophe, and war. The book went through thirteen printings in two years. By 1971, fully 40 percent of Americans believed that the size of the population in the United States was a major problem.[11]

Rockefeller was a veritable crusader against overpopulation, having established the Population Council in 1952 in order to support research into reproduction and deploy demographers around the world.[12] Attempting to tackle both sides of the issue, Rockefeller supported both efforts to expand food production and attempts to limit population growth. Hesburgh enthusiastically embraced the former but was more wary of the latter. When he accepted the invitation to join the board in 1961, he was impressed with the foundation's support for agricultural research, which had produced the genetically modified, high-yielding grains that ushered in the "green revolution" of the 1950s and 1960s. Hesburgh sincerely believed that such scientific advances were the key to ending world hunger.

Hesburgh had greater reservations when it came to controlling population. In 1958, he had convinced an earlier Rockefeller project to drop its recommendation that international aid be conditioned on the adoption of population control measures. He vehemently objected to any coercive "fuller brush" approach that imposed mandatory programs on whole nations or regions. But even optional programs, he knew, too easily drifted into direct conflict with Catholic teaching on contraception, sterilization, and, ultimately, abortion. When Rockefeller asked him to serve on the board, Hesburgh remembered replying: "I know I agree with about ninety percent of what you're doing, but there are some things you're doing that I don't agree with like abortion. Every time it comes up I'm going to vote against it and do what I can to change the policy."[13]

In hindsight, it is fair to say that Hesburgh did not so much change the work of the foundation as the work changed him—if not on abortion, at least when it came to the question of birth control. As a young priest, Hesburgh held a very traditional view of family planning, one that was common among post-war Catholics, namely, that "our big families are our happy families." In a 1947 sermon, Hesburgh complained that young couples were deluged with magazines and other "filthy literature telling them twenty new ways of practicing birth control." The Christian family was "fighting for its life" because so many parents refused to welcome children—or chose to have only one or two children. Like Mary and Joseph, to welcome a child is to welcome Christ: "Whatsoever you did unto one of these my least brethren, you did it unto Me."[14] For years, Hesburgh never questioned the righteousness of the church's position. As late as 1960, when asked why the Catholic Church would not revise its teaching on artificial contraception, as had many Protestant churches, Hesburgh replied, "We cannot reverse our position, because it is based on unchanging philosophical and theological principles regarding the nature and destiny of man, of marriage and of sexuality, too."[15]

Over the next decade, Hesburgh grew increasingly convinced that the church's teaching not only could change but should. The impetus came not from a reconsideration of eternal philosophical and theological principles, but from concerns about overpopulation. Throughout the 1960s, as Hesburgh was confronting racial inequities at home, he was also learning more and more about inequities abroad. He admired the self-help approach of secular foundations, finding them to be more effective than the church's traditional emphasis on charitable giving.[16] He wanted to address the root causes of poverty and hunger. As he later remarked, "it became obvious we had a real problem with population. . . . [Overpopulation] is a terrible strain on economics, education, food [and] housing. . . . I began to see that in the long run [the Catholic Church's position on birth control] was not really a sustainable policy for the good of all humanity. I became more and more unconvinced by the arguments that I myself used when I was teaching the marriage class."[17] In addition to advocating medical research that would improve the effectiveness of natural forms of birth control, Hesburgh also lent his support to a series of conferences at Notre Dame between 1963 and 1967 quietly organized by his special assistant, George Schuster. The purpose of these gatherings was to raise awareness of the population problem among Catholics so as to promote a liberalization of church teaching on artificial contraception.[18]

All of this took place at a time when Hesburgh sincerely believed that an official change in church teaching on contraception was imminent. The reforming spirit of the Second Vatican Council brought a feeling of sweeping change across the Catholic world. Seemingly eternal realities, like the Latin liturgy, were transformed overnight, and the "development of doctrine" became a hot topic among theologians. Like other informed Catholics, Hesburgh knew that Pope John XXIII had created a special papal commission to study the question of birth control, a group that Paul VI extended and enlarged. Through his good friends Pat and Patty Crowley, leaders of the Christian Family Movement who served on that commission, Hesburgh came to know that most of its members recommended a change in church teaching, which he also began to favor. Thus Hesburgh saw his own evolving views as moving with the church, not against it.

And so it was with shock that Hesburgh learned of Pope Paul VI's decision to reaffirm the church's traditional prohibition against all forms of artificial contraception. The pope's controversial encyclical, *Humanae Vitae*, was published on July 25, 1968. "Looking back," writes Stephen Schloesser, "a more ill-advised and ill-timed appearance is difficult to imagine." This was, after all, the "Year that Rocked the World." The encyclical arrived in the midst of an unprecedented global collapse of trust in authority. Ticking off a long list of traumas—from the Tet Offensive, to the assassination of Martin Luther King, Jr., to the riots outside the Democratic National Convention—Schloesser concludes: "In short: the summer of 1968 was an inauspicious moment in which to reassert authority with an unpopular encyclical."[19] And the negative reaction was fierce, marked by an outpouring of disagreement and public criticism of the pope that had never been seen before among American Catholics.

Despite his own reservations, Hesburgh did not publicly dissent from the pope's teaching as did many other prominent Catholics. When a reporter from *Time* magazine asked him, "Do you believe birth control is a sin?" Hesburgh artfully ducked. He replied: "I hope not. I have been practicing it all my life."[20] Deflecting attention away from his own doubt, Hesburgh did not shy away from defending the right of others to disagree. When Father James Burtchaell, CSC, who was then chair of the theology department and soon-to-be the first provost at Notre Dame, denounced *Humanae Vitae* in a lecture on campus ("The Bitter Pill"), the alumni were furious—forcing Hesburgh to respond with a formal press conference. "I'm against half of the stuff that's talked about around here," he told reporters, "but that's irrelevant, because anyone with a mind has to take a stand, and you take it as you wish." He defended the academic freedom of his faculty. He wanted students and their professors to discuss openly the great issues of the day. "That's what we exist for, to look at tough questions and try to find answers. As far as I'm concerned, a university, if it is going to be true to itself, ought to be willing to sit down and confront these things."[21]

In the end, Hesburgh could never accept the distinction *Humanae Vitae* made between "artificial" and "natural" birth control. He believed that "the moment they say that natural birth control—all that cycle stuff—is okay, then they can't say that it is immoral to have sexual relations when conception is impossible."[22] He became increasingly convinced that the pope's decision did real damage to the church, undermining the faith of Catholics in the teaching authority of the pope across the board.

Humanae Vitae also put strain on Hesburgh's personal relationship with Paul VI. In 1969, Hesburgh endorsed comments made by the Belgian Cardinal Leo Josef Suenens that were severely critical of the Vatican. Hesburgh believed that the critique was directed at the pope's advisors and not at the pope himself. So when a friend in Rome, Father Ed Heston, told Hesburgh that some in the pope's inner circle were accusing him of ingratitude and disloyalty, he refused to hear it. "They're confusing disloyalty with honesty. . . . The most loyal thing I can do for the Pope is to be honest with him, as I always have been." When Heston implored him to retract his statement, Hesburgh refused. "I am not going to retract something that I believe to be the truth."[23]

Up until that point, Hesburgh had enjoyed a particularly close relationship with Paul VI. Their friendship went back to 1960, when Hesburgh invited the future pope, Cardinal Giovanni Battista Montini, to Notre Dame to preach at the baccalaureate Mass (Montini was joined that year by President Eisenhower, who gave the commencement address). One of the few who could converse with the cardinal in Italian, Hesburgh showed him around campus, stopping in at each of the residence hall chapels to pray.

Following the visit, Hesburgh stayed in touch with Montini. After the cardinal became pope in 1963, Hesburgh met with him regularly in his capacity as Vatican representative to the International Atomic Energy Agency and as president of the International Federation of Catholic Universities.

When Hesburgh learned that the pope shared his fascination with space travel, he got Jim Webb, the head of NASA, to provide rare photos and films from the Apollo missions. Whenever he was in Rome, Hesburgh brought along these films and watched them with the pope after dinner in the papal residence. Hesburgh remembers the pope watching these movies "with the innocent delight of a little boy."[24]

Inspired by the positive interaction with Protestant and Orthodox observers at the Second Vatican Council, and by his own meeting with the Patriarch Athenagoras in Jerusalem, Pope Paul VI shared with Hesburgh his dream of establishing a research institute in the Holy Land dedicated to promoting Christian unity. He asked Hesburgh for help. Seven years later, thanks to Hesburgh's unswerving commitment and exhausting legwork (as well as the generous support of his benefactor, I. A. O'Shaughnessy), the Tantur Ecumenical Institute opened on a hillside between Jerusalem and Bethlehem.

Tantur was dedicated in 1972. By then, Hesburgh had resigned from the Atomic Energy Agency and stepped down as president of the Federation of Catholic Universities. He had little reason to call on the pope and was perhaps too proud to make amends after their falling out. It wasn't until 1974 that they reconnected. Following a large audience with representatives of the Holy Cross order, Paul VI walked right up to Hesburgh to ask why he never visited any more. "I want to see you," the pope said, "I'm telling you that when you are in Rome, you come to see me." For years after the pope passed away, whenever Hesburgh was in Rome, he stopped to say a prayer at Pope Paul's tomb, wanting to honor the wish of his friend.[25]

Hesburgh's experience in public service and his stout patriotism made it unlikely that he would ever fully remove himself from national concerns. In the wake of Vietnam, one of those concerns was what to do with the thousands of young men who had evaded military service during the war. Pardon or punishment? Clemency or charges? Ushered into office by Nixon's downfall, Gerald R. Ford became president in 1974 with a promise "to bind up the nation's wounds." Out of concern for the future of the country and in a spirit of mercy, Ford extended an unconditional pardon to the former president on September 8, 1974. A week later Ford announced plans to grant conditional amnesty to draft dodgers and deserters of the Vietnam era. Ford asked Hesburgh to serve on the nine-member (later expanded to eighteen) Presidential Clemency Board created to review individual cases.

Earlier Hesburgh had declared himself in favor of full and unconditional amnesty for those evading service during Vietnam. He argued that if those responsible for planning and pursuing the war at the top had escaped with impunity, then why should those caught down in its trenches be punished. His openly liberal attitude toward clemency brought Hesburgh into frequent conflict with the most conservative voice on the board, the retired Marine Corps general Lewis Walt. At an early meeting, Walt announced, "I'm against amnesty, and if one person out of a hundred gets amnesty, I will think we're doing badly."

"Well, if ninety-nine out of a hundred do *not* get amnesty," Hesburgh retorted, "I'm going to think we're doing badly, because I'm in the forgiving business and amnesty means forgiving."[26]

The two men could chat about fishing and hunting over breaks, but they disagreed vehemently during their meetings—at times threatening the mission of the board. One observer recalled that they were "both men of strong will and immense self-discipline."[27] In the end, Hesburgh played a decisive role in persuading his colleagues to adopt a more lenient approach. Drawing on his experience with the Civil Rights Commission, he also helped the board confront racial disparities in sentencing, forcing the group to recognize that, far too often, black offenders had received more severe penalties than white offenders. With the other members of the board, Hesburgh spent most of the summer of 1975 in Washington, working at a feverish pace to review more than one hundred cases a day. At the end of their year of service, the board had granted some form of clemency to all but 911 of the 15,468 cases they considered.[28]

Hesburgh knew that the 15,468 who had applied for clemency represented only a fraction of the nearly 100,000 who were still eligible. Working with his contacts at the Ford Foundation, he created a task force to research and develop a plan for handling the remaining cases. Shortly after Jimmy Carter was elected, Hesburgh and the head of the Ford Foundation, McGeorge Bundy, presented the president-elect with their plan. On his first day in office, President Carter put their plan into action by granting an unconditional pardon to all those who had evaded the draft during the Vietnam War.

Hesburgh felt comfortable approaching Carter because Carter had already approached him. A few months earlier, in the thick of the campaign, Jimmy Carter called Hesburgh around nine thirty Sunday night from his kitchen in Plains, Georgia, to ask Hesburgh's advice: Why was he having such a hard time connecting with Catholics? Hesburgh told Carter that his big problem was abortion, and that it was a mistake to have come out against the constitutional amendment being proposed by the US Catholic bishops. His argument to the candidate was not moral but pragmatic: The president has no control over constitutional amendments, so Carter shouldn't put himself in the middle of a debate "when there was no reason for him to be there."[29] This politically savvy move deeply disappointed Hesburgh's younger confrere and biographer, William Miscamble, CSC, who saw in the exchange an effort to minimize the abortion issue. In discussing the topic, Hesburgh "did not address it as a priest who saw abortion as a moral blight on the United States that should be ended." Instead he "treated the issue as one to be circumvented."[30]

Miscamble complained that Hesburgh did not do enough to end abortion, that he did not speak out more forcefully—not only on the phone with Carter, but throughout his long career. Yet, even Miscamble acknowledged that the Notre Dame president was not silent on the matter. For example, in his 1973 Yale lectures, delivered less than twelve months after *Roe v. Wade*, Hesburgh called attention to "those who have no voice at all, the unborn children who are so cavalierly deprived of the most basic right of all, the right to life"—a line that drew hisses from his Ivy League audience.[31]

Throughout the 1980s, Hesburgh offered concrete proposals for reducing what he called the moral "abomination" of abortion. He repeatedly described a sign he once saw hanging above a cemetery in Hong Kong, which read, "What you are I once was; what I am you soon will be." Hesburgh observed that a fetus could very well say to us: "What I am you once were. What you are I soon will be, if you let me."[32]

If Hesburgh consistently went on record against abortion, it seems that Miscamble's real problem with Hesburgh was that he hung out with the wrong kind of people. For Miscamble, Hesburgh fraternized with the enemy, associating himself with the pro-abortion, liberal elites running things at the Rockefeller and Ford Foundations. As Kenneth Woodward put it, Miscamble doesn't like the fact that "this American priest ate with sinners."[33]

Miscamble's charge—one-sided as it is—is nevertheless important because it brings to light the very heart of Hesburgh's approach to the world. Hesburgh saw himself as a mediator, a bridge builder who chose dialogue over denunciation, critical engagement over outright boycott. Reasonable people, he was convinced, could find common ground if they only met one another with respect and argued their positions with civility. When he was booed at Yale, Hesburgh paused and remained silent until the hissing died down. He then admonished the audience: "I don't mind at all that you disagree with me, but to hiss because I say something that you don't agree with, well that strikes me as not worthy of a great university." We need to be able to "disagree without being disagreeable."[34] Hesburgh had little patience for uncritical ideologues at either extreme. The following year, he told a gathering of the Catholic Press Association that pro-life advocates had to be "effectively concerned and thoughtfully articulate about abortion, not backing unworkable solutions, not engaging in calling the opposition murderers, not being politically naïve." Many "forces for good" did not want to be associated with "mindless and crude zealots who have neither good judgment, sophistication of procedure, nor the modicum of civility needed for the rational discussion of disagreements in a pluralistic democracy."[35]

A decade later, when New York Governor Mario Cuomo gave his landmark speech arguing that Catholic politicians who personally opposed abortion could still support the right of a woman to choose one, Hesburgh's response was measured. Cuomo came to Notre Dame in the middle of the 1984 presidential campaign at the invitation of Hesburgh's close friend and collaborator, Father Richard McBrien, chair of the theology department. Hesburgh defended giving Cuomo a platform at Notre Dame and even called his talk "brilliant."

Yet, in a thoughtful essay published after the event, Hesburgh argued for an alternate middle course. He compared *Roe v. Wade* to *Plessy v. Ferguson*, the 1896 Supreme Court decision that upheld racial segregation. Like *Roe*, *Plessy v. Ferguson* was a mistake. It was only finally overturned when enough people came to realize its fundamental injustice. "Neither the consensus nor the change just happened; both were made to happen." Hesburgh saw his fifteen years on the Civil Rights Commission as an effort to build an even broader consensus against the unjust treatment of African Americans. The pro-life movement is called to a similar task of building consensus. And it begins with the "secret consensus" that already exists: Most Americans favor greater limitations on abortion, even if they do not support an outright ban. "But generally, the pro-life movement has been for an absolute prohibition of abortion. If such a total solution is not possible in our pluralistic society, will Catholics cooperate with other Americans of good will and ethical conviction to work for a more restrictive abortion law?" One would hope so, Hesburgh concluded. Then, Catholic politicians would not feel compelled to say, "I'm against abortion, but . . ." Instead, they could even "relive the civil rights revolution in the ultimate context of life and death."[36]

Although he disagreed with Carter on abortion, Hesburgh liked the Georgia governor and strongly endorsed his human rights approach to foreign policy. The esteem was mutual. After he was elected, Carter asked Hesburgh to suggest people the president-elect ought to consider for senior appointments in the administration. Hesburgh claimed that nearly half of the one hundred names he submitted went on to work for the new president. When Carter spoke at Notre Dame's commencement in 1977, he praised Hesburgh's twenty-five years of service, saying that Father Hesburgh had "spoken more consistently and more effectively in support of the rights of human beings than any other person I know."[37]

On that visit, Carter asked Hesburgh to lead the US delegation to a United Nations Conference on Science and Technology for Development scheduled to take place in 1979 in Vienna. In agreeing, Hesburgh accepted the rank of ambassador, the first for a US Catholic priest. Hesburgh found this combination of roles not only acceptable but also appropriate. An ambassador is called to serve as a go-between—a bridge—between nations and groups. An ambassador is a mediator, which is the very heart of the priestly vocation.[38] Carter continued to ask the priestly bridge-builder for assistance. He added Hesburgh to the President's Commission on the Holocaust, a group chaired by Elie Wiesel and charged with recommending an appropriate national memorial. And in 1979, Carter appointed Hesburgh chair of the Select Commission on Immigration and Refugee Policy—a group that soon became known as the "Hesburgh Commission."

In many ways, Hesburgh's eighteen months heading up the Select Commission on Immigration offers a microcosm of this chapter of his life. This was not Hesburgh's most consequential assignment, but it contained many of the elements that had come to characterize his life of public service. Here was another opportunity for Hesburgh to work for the good of the country by playing a leading role in drawing together people with diverse views in order to tackle an intractable problem with deep moral implications.

The scope of the problem was clear: At the time of his appointment, Hesburgh argued, immigration "was massively out of control."[39] While the law allowed for the US to receive 230,000 immigrants annually, up to 2 million were entering the country illegally every year. An additional 800,000 to 900,000 came as political refugees. The moral dimension was obvious: Anywhere from 6 to 12 million undocumented immigrants lived in the United States, with uncertain status, few rights, vulnerable to discrimination, exploitation, and family strife, and always fearful of deportation. The divergence of views was wide: Business interests lined up against labor, civil rights groups against law enforcement. The need for a skilled mediator was keen: The commission was comprised of four public members; four senators, two from each party; four members of the House of Representatives, two from each party; the Secretary of State, Secretary of Labor, Secretary of Health and Human Services, and the Attorney General. The work was intense: Over the course of eighteen months, the commission held public hearings in twelve major points of entry to the United States—from New York to San Francisco to San Antonio— and produced reports and recommendations that filled thirteen thick volumes. This was the kind of public service that had become Hesburgh's hallmark. Even his unfailing faith in technological progress is evident in his recommendation (ultimately voted down by the commission) to issue plastic identity cards with embedded microchips to all citizens and legal residents in order to guard against the illegal hiring of undocumented workers.

In advising President Carter to appoint Hesburgh to take the place of Reubin Askew as chair of the Commission on Immigration, White House personnel director Arnie Miller argued that the "Commission Chairman must have the stature and prestige to command the respect and involvement of Cabinet officers and Members of Congress and possess the leadership necessary to build a workable consensus about the immigration issue." In addition to meeting all these criteria, Miller believed that Hesburgh would provide "strong moral leadership" to the group. Clearly, President Carter agreed.[40]

While Hesburgh was leading the Commission on Immigration, he also spearheaded efforts to respond to a humanitarian disaster unfolding in Cambodia. From 1975 to 1979, that country suffered horrifically under the brutal dictator Pol Pot, whose Khmer Rouge regime killed over a million of its own people (some estimates put the number at more than two and a half million deaths—approximately a quarter of the population). A Vietnamese attack in December 1978 opened a window into the "killing fields" of Cambodia and intensified an already dire refugee crisis. Tens of thousands of Cambodians fled to the border with Thailand, where they were denied entry. Over the coming months, the world watched as thousands of refugees died of starvation and disease.

At the time, Hesburgh was still serving as chair of the Overseas Development Council. With the help of James Grant, president of the ODC, Hesburgh convened a group of forty religious and relief organization leaders to respond to the crisis. They gathered on the morning of October 24, 1979, at their DC headquarters. Within two hours they had agreed on a coordinated relief plan. Hesburgh contacted the White House, and later that day the group met with President Carter in the Cabinet Room. With Hesburgh at his side, Carter pledged $69 million in immediate assistance to the relief effort. Hesburgh partnered with the president's wife, Rosalynn Carter, to raise public awareness. He became cochair of the National Cambodian Crisis Committee, an umbrella organization created to raise money for refugees. The following July, Hesburgh joined James Grant to tour relief efforts in Cambodia and to lobby King Bhumibol of Thailand to lift controls at the border. When the king tried to blame "political" obstacles to solving the refugee problem, Hesburgh was direct: "[W]hen politics rise above humanitarianism, then civilization faces disaster." After the king complained that Hesburgh was essentially accusing him of insanity, the priest replied, "there was another kind of insanity with which I agreed, namely, being just and right, no matter what the opposition or the criticism."

Those traveling with Hesburgh were struck by the "saintly anger" he directed toward the Pol Pot regime, which he compared to the brutality of the Third Reich. They were also impressed with the sheer stamina of the sixty-three-year-old priest. One reporter wrote, "Father Hesburgh . . . doesn't complain of the length of the journey or of the chaos, thirst or lack of food provisions. He only expresses admiration for the wounded Kampuchean people and his indignation as we cross devastated towns and villages." When critics in the US accused Hesburgh of cooperating with America's recent enemy, the Communist Vietnamese, in distributing relief supplies, he answered them: "When someone is hungry, you don't ask him what his political beliefs are, you give him something to eat."[41] Although Miscamble suggests that Hesburgh may have exaggerated the impact he had on Cambodia: "Still, he had influenced the Carter administration to act, and he led the American private aid effort to raise funding for Cambodia with those crucial humanitarian purposes in mind. It was a stellar performance."[42]

Hesburgh would ultimately judge Jimmy Carter "a terrible manager" and an ineffective president. Nonetheless he appreciated the president's efforts toward peace in the Middle East, rapprochement with the Soviet Union, and a foreign policy strongly committed to human rights. However, the warm relationship that Hesburgh enjoyed with the occupant of the Oval Office would not continue under Carter's successor.

On the surface, the election of Ronald Reagan would seem to have been a boon for the president of the University of Notre Dame. As a young actor, Reagan had played the role of Notre Dame's legendary halfback George Gipp in the 1940 film *Knute Rockne, All American*. The film made famous Gipp's dying words to "win one for the Gipper." Reagan had visited campus in May 1940 for the filming and returned to South Bend that October for the premier. However, despite the connection between Reagan the actor and Notre Dame, no real relationship formed between Reagan the president and Hesburgh.

Shortly after Reagan's election, Hesburgh extended an invitation to speak at commencement, which was quickly accepted. The charismatic president came to Notre Dame on May 17, 1981—his first major speech outside Washington since the assassination attempt by John Hinckley in March. Security was tight and the visit was tense. Reagan was on campus for less than three hours, and Hesburgh was only able to exchange pleasantries with the president. The speech Reagan delivered, however, gave Hesburgh a lot to mull over.

Reagan played up the Gipper connection, but then turned to two of the major concerns that would guide his presidency: limiting the federal government's role at home and confronting the communist threat abroad. On both issues, Hesburgh had staked out decidedly different positions. His work on the Civil Rights Commission convinced him that the federal government had an indispensable role to play in promoting the common good—particularly on issues of injustice that were not being addressed at the local level. Furthermore, his work with the International Atomic Energy Agency persuaded Hesburgh that greater cooperation, not confrontation, was the path toward peace between the nuclear powers.

It was on the nuclear issue that Hesburgh grew increasingly concerned. Hesburgh had always been a fierce critic of communism, with its atheistic foundation and totalitarian impulses. Yet Reagan's hardline approach toward the Soviet Union was fundamentally at odds with Hesburgh's own commitment to dialogue and reconciliation.

The urgency of the nuclear arms race hit home for Hesburgh that fall. November 11, 1981 was designated "Nuclear Day" at college campuses around the country. Hesburgh presided at a special Mass and preached against the nuclear danger. He then listened to a lecture by Notre Dame alumnus Dr. James Muller, Harvard professor and cofounder of Physicians for Social Responsibility, an antinuclear organization. Muller described in vivid detail the effects that a one-megaton nuclear bomb would have if it were detonated over Notre Dame's campus. As he walked back to his office alone, Hesburgh remembered having a kind of epiphany: "[I]t suddenly occurred to me that all the good things I had been working on during the past thirty years were irrelevant if we did not solve this problem. Civil rights, world hunger, development in the Third World, education, immigration and refugees, illiteracy, housing, health—all of these would be irrelevant if there were no more human beings left to have problems. All the progress I had worked so hard for could be obliterated in a few minutes if the nuclear weapons, now existing, were unleashed."[43]

Hesburgh had long known about the dangers of the Cold War. But something about Muller's warning seized him in a new way. He dropped almost everything—resigning from his positions at the Rockefeller Foundation, the Overseas Development Council, and other boards—in order to focus his energies on what he soon described as an existential threat to the human race.

Hesburgh began by contacting Cardinal Franz König in Vienna, with whom he had worked while at the IAEA, in order to organize church forces against the nuclear threat. The US Catholic bishops, under the leadership of Archbishop Joseph Bernardin, had already begun the process of drafting a pastoral statement on war and peace. Approved in 1983, after a lengthy consultative process that involved public hearings and multiple drafts, *The Challenge of Peace* took issue with the massive nuclear build-up under Reagan. Hesburgh endorsed the bishops' work wholeheartedly. He lectured around the country, calling nuclear war a blasphemy, the worst sin since Creation. In the audience of one of these lectures was a woman whom Hesburgh did not know, who came up afterward and said to him, "I really believe in what you're doing and I'm going to help you." The woman was Joan Kroc, the wealthy widow of Ray Kroc, founder of the McDonald's fast-food chain, and that lecture led to gifts, eventually totaling over $60 million, to support a center for peace studies at Notre Dame.[44]

Hesburgh's greatest contribution to peacemaking, however, was his work of mediation. Hesburgh decided to bring together scientists and religious leaders in order to speak with a united voice. He raised $100,000 for his campaign, "Science and Religion Against Nuclear War," sponsoring a series of meetings in Vienna, London, the Vatican, and elsewhere, between 1982 and 1984. The highpoint of these efforts was a six-hundred-word statement signed by representatives from the five major nuclear powers (China, France, Great Britain, the Soviet Union, and the United States) and several other countries. The statement condemned nuclear war, laid out the calamitous effects of "nuclear winter," and called for action: "Our central purpose and proximate endeavor must be to reduce international tensions (particularly between the Soviet Union and the United States), to develop more effective cooperative efforts for dealing with our common human problems and interest, and to bring a great measure of justice and peace to the whole world."[45] Hesburgh lobbied the Reagan administration hard, writing to senators and advisors and even meeting with Vice President George Bush to discuss the issue. But despite his efforts, he never got access to the president.

For Hesburgh, the nuclear issue was not just a military or a political issue: it was at root a moral and a spiritual issue. In his speeches and essays he often appealed to the theological principle of reconciliation. We need to learn how "to sit down and talk with the Russians, to try to draw their humanity out of them . . . and have them see that we are all up against a common evil."[46] Was Hesburgh naïve in his efforts to promote peace among the world powers through dialogue? Perhaps. But it is hard to deny the sincerity of his efforts or the energy he brought to the cause. As was the case with so many of Hesburgh's contributions, his approach to peacemaking rested on his deep conviction that people separated by vast differences can come together in their shared humanity and meet one another at the personal level, if only they have a bridge builder.

If, prior to Hesburgh's tenure as president of the university, Notre Dame was best known for its football coach Knute Rockne, by the end of his tenure it is fair to say that Notre Dame was known for its priest-president Father Ted Hesburgh. His contributions off campus equaled, and may have even exceeded, his contributions on campus. "Somewhere in the 70s, there was a turning point where he just passed into the hall of fame," reflected Notre Dame professor Frederick Crosson.[47] Across a range of major issues, Hesburgh provided a steady hand and a consistent moral voice throughout one of the most tumultuous periods in American history. Columnist Colman McCarthy called Hesburgh "one of the few idealists we have who aren't being ground down by the times."[48] His confidence in humanity's goodness was unending and his energy was inexhaustible. When asked *why? Why take on so much?* Hesburgh replied, "You've got to have meaning in your life. You've got to get up in the morning with some sense that today is not going to be just an exercise in drudgery or routine, but something is going to happen because you're living that day. . . . Meaning in life comes from making a difference."[49]

CHAPTER SEVEN

To the End

Hesburgh became president of the University of Notre Dame at age thirty-five, a position he held for the next thirty-five years. In 1987, at the age of seventy, he stepped down as president. But he hardly retired. For the next three decades, Hesburgh remained actively engaged in pastoral ministry, the life of the nation, and the work of the university. In excellent health, and as energetic and optimistic as ever, he entered what would be the last third of his life with a commitment to seek out new ways to serve God, country, and Notre Dame. Always looking forward, Hesburgh titled the final chapter of his autobiography "Starting the Future."

Hesburgh began that future with a year away from the campus he loved. He decided that the best gift he could give to his successor, Father Edward "Monk" Malloy, CSC, was to disappear for a while so that the new administration could assume leadership on their own terms. His parting advice to Monk was: "Be yourself."[1]

Together with his faithful friend and right-hand man, Father Ned Joyce, who served as his executive vice president for all thirty-five years, Hesburgh planned a ten-month trip around the world. It began with—of all things—a tour of the western United States in a borrowed RV.

Friends and family had their doubts about these two bachelors heading out on their own. "I don't think he knows how to take care of himself," said Hesburgh's sister. "He doesn't know how to cook, as far as I know. The secretaries have been taking care of him and Father Joyce for so long."[2] The running joke was that the two wouldn't make it past Gary, Indiana, seventy miles to the west. So as they waved goodbye and pulled away from campus in their enormous home-on-wheels, towing a small Chevy behind them, Hesburgh held a sign to the window for all to see. It read: "GARY OR BUST."

"Never had two more innocent persons taken to the road in an RV," Hesburgh wrote in his travel journal. "Although Ned had been given some instructions by the Skyline people in nearby Elkhart, I had seen the vehicle only once or twice before and knew absolutely nothing about it. That explains in part why Ned was driving. Not wanting to be completely useless, I prayed the Breviary—out loud so it counted for both of us."[3]

Ted and Ned made it past Gary, through Chicago, and on to the great open plains and the rugged beauty of the Rocky Mountains, which Hesburgh described in his journal with loving detail. Over the next two-and-a-half months, they toured seventeen national parks and twenty-nine national forests, connecting with Notre Dame alumni and old friends all along the way. They squeezed into their small bunks, figured out how to cook in the tiny kitchen on board, and navigated laundromats for the first time. According to Hesburgh's recollection, they managed just fine and had a great time with it.

Shortly after their western adventures, the two men continued their sabbatical aboard the *Queen Elizabeth 2*, first with a three-week cruise of the Caribbean and then a three-month trip across the world. They sailed to New Zealand, Australia, and Mombasa in East Africa, and then back across the Pacific, stopping in China, Korea, Japan, and Hawaii. During their more than one hundred days at sea, the two priests earned their keep by serving as ship chaplains. They celebrated daily Mass for Catholic passengers, organized Christmas caroling, responded to spiritual and personal crises (including an attempted suicide on board), and engaged in regular, informal pastoral counseling. One afternoon, Hesburgh spent over an hour comforting a member of the cleaning staff in Spanish. After another conversation, he wrote in his journal: "It's amazing how many stories are packed into a ship like this, how many tragedies, and how many opportunities."[4]

Upon returning to Notre Dame, Hesburgh moved into a new office on the thirteenth floor of the library he had built, recently renamed in his honor by the Board of Trustees. In this space, with its panoramic view of campus and "bookshelves from floor to ceiling," Hesburgh got right back to work.[5] With the help of the Chicago writer Jerry Reedy, he compiled his memoirs, *God, Country, Notre Dame*, which was published in 1990 and sold over half a million copies. Two years later came *Travels with Ted & Ned*, based on Hesburgh's journal from their year on the road and at sea. This was followed in 1994 by a collection Hesburgh edited, *The Challenge and Promise of a Catholic University*.

Alongside his writing projects, Hesburgh was a frequent guest lecturer on campus, invited into undergraduate classrooms to share stories from his time on the Civil Rights Commission, or to discuss US-Soviet relations during the Cold War, or to answer questions about what it was like to work with JFK and LBJ. Most weekends, Hesburgh would celebrate late-night Mass for students in the residence halls. During the week, if his secretary Helen Hosinski was away from the office, the priest would famously wander out into the library stacks, find some unsuspecting student studying, and draft her or him to read the Scriptures for the daily Mass he was about to celebrate in his private chapel.

In *God, Country, Notre Dame*, Hesburgh outlined the "five ideas" that he wanted to work on in his retirement: (1) peace in a nuclear age; (2) human rights and justice worldwide; (3) human development in the Third World; (4) ecology and environmental advocacy; and (5) ecumenism and interreligious dialogue. These ideas continued trajectories Hesburgh had set during his tenure as president. The first three he saw as inextricably intertwined—since "there can be no peace in the world without human rights and equitable development of the resources we all have to live with." But as the Cold War fear of mutual nuclear destruction faded, Hesburgh argued in 1990, we have to "turn the full force of our attention and ingenuity to the even broader task of preserving our own habitat, our own environment."[6] Moreover, he believed that little progress would be made on any of these already demanding tasks if religion continued to divide humanity rather than unite it. As president, Hesburgh had established special institutes at Notre Dame to address each of these five challenges. Although Hesburgh no longer weighed in on the day-to-day operations of the university and was rarely consulted by his successor (a sore point for Hesburgh), he remained actively involved on the advisory boards of these institutes—discussing programs with the staff and helping with recruitment and fundraising.

For many years into retirement Hesburgh kept up the work day rhythm he had established as president. He slept late, arrived at the library around noon, rode the elevator to the eighth floor, and then, for exercise, took the last five flights of stairs to his office. He worked all afternoon, broke for dinner, and returned to the office—often handling correspondence or reading reports until well past two o'clock in the morning. He always said that he would "rather wear out than rust out" and he kept busy.[7]

When away from campus, Hesburgh made the most of his time. Michael O'Brien reports on one twenty-four-hour period not long after he retired: Hesburgh "spoke about the nuclear arms race to the Notre Dame Club of Delaware in Wilmington on Wednesday evening; the following day he addressed students at a Wilmington high school, talked with six seniors about to enter Notre Dame, was interviewed on television, and visited the Wilmington Free Library where he read stories to a group of preschoolers."[8] In the spring of 1990, Hesburgh was invited to speak at fifteen different college commencements, but could only attend four. He just did not have the time.

In 1991, Hesburgh was appointed to the Board of Directors of the US Institute of Peace, his fifteenth presidential appointment. (His sixteenth and final presidential appointment would come in 2001.) A 1994 résumé lists membership on over fifty boards and committees. Some of these positions were largely honorary, but several involved a significant commitment of time and energy. For example, in 1989 Hesburgh agreed to cochair the Knight Commission on Intercollegiate Athletics with his friend William Friday, former president of the University of North Carolina. Established in the wake of major scandals in college athletics, the commission worked for over three years to propose a number of financial and academic reforms. Approximately 65 percent of these proposals were ultimately adopted by the NCAA. Although Hesburgh was not a big sports fan, he agreed to serve as cochair because, he said, "I don't want to see athletics tarnish the institution I love, the American University."[9]

A year after starting work on the Knight Commission, Hesburgh was elected to a six-year term on the Harvard University Board of Overseers—the first priest ever to join this elite group. They ultimately chose Hesburgh as board chair in 1994. That fall, when the university president, Neil Rudenstine, suffered a nervous breakdown caused by overwork, Hesburgh rose to the occasion. He immediately met with Rudenstine, appointed an interim, and calmed the board by bringing in the president's physician and dean of the medical school to answer questions. He laid out a plan to get the president some rest, adjust his schedule, and transition him back to work. "The board of overseers seemed reassured by the guarantees of the elderly priest, and the crisis surrounding Rudenstine's leadership of Harvard soon subsided." Hesburgh "played a crucial role in steadying the Harvard ship," and the board recognized his leadership by electing Hesburgh to a rare second term as chair.[10]

Less laudatory was Hesburgh's decision in 1994 to cochair a legal defense fund for President Bill Clinton and First Lady Hillary Clinton. The fund was established to cover legal expenses from lawsuits going back to Clinton's time as governor of Arkansas. Since his days on the Civil Rights Commission, Hesburgh's progressive leanings were clear; however, he was a political independent and always claimed to be nonpartisan. Critics accused him of abandoning that neutrality in taking up such a politically charged assignment. Hesburgh, who always had a special respect for the office of the president, responded that he agreed to do this for the sake of the *presidency*, not for this particular president. Later, following the scandals that led to Clinton's impeachment, Hesburgh had to admit, "I would say the whole thing was one of the most unproductive things I was ever involved in."[11]

All the while he served on these national and international committees, Hesburgh continued to speak out on issues facing church and society. He had great respect for Pope John Paul II's defense of human rights around the world as well as for his efforts to promote greater interreligious understanding. However, Hesburgh was bothered by the Polish pope's impatience with dissenting views and his inflexibility on internal church matters. On the eve of John Paul II's 1987 visit to the United States, Hesburgh penned an open letter to the Holy Father calling for a more open, and mutual, dialogue.

Addressing the pope, he wrote: "It is good and generous of you to travel the whole world to speak to millions of people, to make your person known to them. . . . Might I suggest that they also would like to make themselves, their hopes and their fears, known to you?" Hesburgh continued, "You will meet with the bishops and speak with them. Will they have a chance to speak freely with you? . . . Then there are our priests. . . . You spoke to them, but they did not have a chance to speak with you, frankly and openly." Hesburgh went on to list various groups: university leaders, married couples, young people, theologians, doctors, lawyers, journalists, and business people. "You have addressed all of them on many occasions. They would honestly like to address you." Women religious have not been heard. Lay women, too, are "a very special group, probably more articulate and more concerned than almost any group in our society. . . . Would they like to be heard? None more."[12]

As the Vatican undertook a comprehensive review of the Code of Canon Law in the early 1980s, Hesburgh lobbied hard, but unsuccessfully, for changes that would reflect the vision of Catholic higher education he had helped to shape, particularly through his contributions to the Land O'Lakes Statement and the 1973 document, *The Catholic University in the Modern World*. He objected strenuously to Pope John

Paul II's efforts, through both the new Code and his 1990 apostolic constitution *Ex Corde Ecclesiae*, to impose juridical norms on Catholic universities. Hesburgh saw juridical requirements, such as the expectation that Catholic theologians obtain a *mandatum* (mandate) from their local bishop, as a threat to the academic freedom he had fought so hard to defend. He felt that such efforts not only ignored the distinctive characteristics of American higher education, but also failed to appreciate his own achievement in building Notre Dame into a great Catholic university.

Hesburgh's frustration with the next generation of leadership came out, in a different way, in a 2001 essay he published in the *Chronicle of Higher Education*, "Where Are College Presidents' Voices on Important Public Issues?" In it, Hesburgh contrasted his own cohort of presidential peers with the current crop of university leaders: "Where we once had a fellowship of public intellectuals, do we now have insulated chief executives intent on keeping the complicated machinery of American higher education running smoothly?" He acknowledged the many pressures contemporary presidents faced, but lamented the rise of managerial-minded, risk-adverse leaders content to "cultivate their own gardens."

His call for greater engagement was at root a call for community. The reason that he and other presidents like him—John Hannah of Michigan State, Bill Friday of UNC, Jim Perkins of Cornell, Katherine McBride of Bryn Mawr— could speak out so forcefully was because they knew one another and knew that they had one another's support. "College presidents may be less present to the American public today because they are less present to one another." Greater community, Hesburgh implied, fosters greater commitment to causes that matter. For him, the lesson of his generation was simple: "We cannot urge students to have the courage to speak out unless we are willing to do so ourselves. The true antidote to the public's view that colleges are simply ivory towers . . . is engagement with important public issues—however difficult and thorny those issues may be."[13]

Awards and honors streamed in. Having received the Presidential Medal of Freedom from Lyndon Johnson in 1964, Hesburgh was awarded the Congressional Gold Medal in 1999 for his "outstanding and enduring contributions to civil rights, higher education, the Catholic Church, the nation, and the global community." In 2002, the University of San Diego granted Hesburgh his 150th honorary degree. (He had already overtaken King Bhumibol of Thailand to claim the world record for most honorary degrees received.) In 2012 Prime Minister Enda Kenny conferred Irish citizenship on Hesburgh. The following year, fulfilling a lifelong dream, Hesburgh was named an honorary chaplain in the US Navy. The ninety-five-year-old priest brought down the house when he told an auditorium of midshipmen, "I hope I will continue to serve the Navy as well as our country in every way possible. Anchors aweigh."[14]

On May 2013, Hesburgh celebrated his ninety-sixth birthday, and seventy years as a priest, in the Rayburn Room of the US Capitol. The party was cohosted by House Speaker John Boehner and Minority Leader Nancy Pelosi and drew lawmakers from both sides of the aisle.[15] The two members of Indiana's split-party Senate delegation were there, along with Vice President Joe Biden, Ambassador Tim Roemer, other members of Congress, church leaders, and Notre Dame officials. The National Portrait Gallery loaned the gathering the famous picture, now part of its permanent collection, of Hesburgh and Martin Luther King, Jr., linked arm in arm, singing "We Shall Overcome" at a Chicago rally. Earlier in the day, Hesburgh had visited with President Barack Obama at the White House—a final and moving exchange between a charter member of the US Civil Rights Commission and the nation's first African American president.

When President Obama spoke at Notre Dame's commencement in May 2009, he shared the story of how Hesburgh brought the six members of the Civil Rights Commission to his retreat at Land O'Lakes and then brought them together around a shared love of fishing. In doing so, Hesburgh helped to bridge their differences, enabling the commission to speak with a common voice for racial justice. The lesson, the president told graduates, is to "remember that in the end, in some way, we are all fishermen."[16]

The decision to invite Obama to Notre Dame drew intense criticism from pro-life advocates, fueling protests, prayer vigils, and even a counter-rally during the ceremony. Hesburgh watched with dismay as this opportunity for dialogue became a source of division. In a letter to the editor of *Notre Dame Magazine*, he situated the controversy squarely within his vision of the moral purpose and proper role of a Catholic university. He wrote: "This year's commencement was indeed 'a defining moment' for Notre Dame because we didn't duck the big issue of our times and the horrendous fact of so many millions of unborn children being coldly killed that brought this to a head. I trust that all of this will have an effect on the national debate and, hopefully, we will see greater efforts to, at least for now, lower the number of abortions and come up with positive programs to help unfortunate women who find themselves in this difficult situation."[17] These words would satisfy neither the extreme right nor the extreme left; nevertheless, they represent Hesburgh's lifelong commitments: the inviolable dignity of the human person, the importance of open debate, and the power of rational persuasion. They reveal his genuine faith that good people can come together to address the world's most pressing problems.

When Hesburgh was awarded the Congressional Gold Medal, an earlier president, Bill Clinton, briefly recounted the extraordinary life that was being recognized with the nation's highest civilian honor. But rather than list Hesburgh's impressive accomplishments, the president spoke of the priest's simple acts of ministry. He concluded that those who knew Father Hesburgh knew that "the most important thing about you and the greatest honor you will ever wear around your neck is the collar you have worn for 57 years."[18]

Father Ted was a priest. He lived through epochal change in church and society, adapting and improvising and evolving as a person. But his commitment to the priesthood—the centrality of it to his very being—never wavered. He knew he wanted to be a priest at the age of six. The one word he asked be engraved on his tombstone was "Priest." On the first page of his autobiography, he wrote: "I want nothing else, have never wanted anything else, never *been* anything else but a priest. I say this now so that you, the reader, will know where I am coming from as you read the thoughts and events of my life."[19]

Given his profound devotion to the priesthood, Hesburgh was deeply, deeply pained by the revelations of clergy sexual abuse that exploded throughout the Catholic Church in 2002. Beginning in Boston and quickly spreading around the world, the abuse crisis brought to light decades of dark secrets—horrific abuse by priests and outrageous efforts by church officials to cover it up.

Though shocked by the extent of the abuse, it was not the first time Hesburgh had heard of priests who would so grievously violate their sacred vocation. His Holy Cross confrere, Father James Burtchaell—who served as Hesburgh's first provost from 1970 to 1977—was removed from ministry in 1991 following an investigation into charges of sexual misconduct with male Notre Dame students. According to Miscamble's account, early into Burtchaell's tenure as provost Hesburgh heard rumors about his behavior, confronted him directly about it, but accepted Burtchaell's denials, taking him at his word that these rumors were a "fabrication" designed to undermine his role at the university. In hindsight, Hesburgh told Miscamble, he realized that he "should have been tougher." But he was adamant that he never tried to conceal inappropriate behavior in order to protect Burtchaell. "I did what I thought was proper to do at the time."[20] Burtchaell—who was clearly being groomed to succeed Hesburgh—was summarily dismissed as provost by the Board of Trustees in 1977, a decision that Hesburgh supported. However, Burtchaell continued to teach at Notre Dame until he was removed from ministry over a decade later.

Another case involved Father Robert Huneke, a diocesan priest from Rockville Centre who served as a resident hall rector in the mid-1970s. In 1996, one of the students abused by Huneke, John Salveson, happened to see Hesburgh on a train from Washington to Baltimore, and took the empty seat next to him. As soon as Hesburgh learned that Salveson was an alum, the retired priest-president began to regale him with stories about Notre Dame. Eventually, Salveson decided to share his own story. As Hesburgh listened intently, his demeanor completely changed. "He looked to me to be angry and disturbed," Salveson remembered. "When I finished my story, he told me he wished I had come to him when I was a student. He said he would have removed the priest immediately."[21] In a *Notre Dame Magazine* article that recounted his experience, Salveson described a nine-year battle to have his abuser removed from ministry after the priest returned to Long Island in the 1980s. Salveson wrote about the failure of his bishop to respond, the resistance he encountered from the diocese, and the revictimization he suffered. "Through it all, the church in which I grew up, the Roman Catholic Church, treated me like the enemy. No one ever apologized for what their priest did to me."

When the train arrived at Baltimore, Hesburgh retrieved his travel bag from the overhead compartment, shook Salveson's hand, and started to walk down the aisle. About halfway off the train, he stopped, turned around and came back to Salveson. Hesburgh said, "If no one has said it to you, I apologize for what happened to you." It was a small gesture, hardly enough to heal the wounds. But Salveson was consoled: "No one had ever said that to me. To this day, he remains the only priest who has said it. It meant more to me than he will ever know."[22]

In the closing pages of his autobiography, Hesburgh wrote that one of the greatest heresies in our modern world is the cynical view that "one person cannot make a difference." He sincerely believed that we *can* change the world, one encounter at a time. His faith in God and in other people was a source of enduring hope. "We all suffer doses of discouragement and disillusionment, but those are distractions for the most part, not driving forces."[23]

Hesburgh's unrelenting optimism for the future held strong, even as his body grew weak. When the aging priest started to have problems with his legs, he exercised on a stationary bicycle every day, while simultaneously trying to learn Chinese. (He claimed that he put over three thousand miles on the bike but didn't get very far with the language. "I learned that when you're past 70 you're not going to learn

Chinese."[24]) When his failing eyesight made it too difficult to read his breviary, he prayed three rosaries a day instead. As the macular degeneration progressed, leaving the voracious reader almost completely blind, a corps of Notre Dame students signed up to take turns reading to him. No longer counseling presidents or popes, Hesburgh enjoyed taking on the role of "everybody's grandfather." As the kinetic priest began to slow down, his personal credo became: "Do as much as you can, as well as you can, as long as you can, and don't complain about the things you can no longer do."[25]

Following a fall in 2004, which opened a cut in his head that required stitches, Hesburgh decided it was finally time to move out of the little room in Corby Hall where he had lived for fifty-three years (right above the dumpster, he liked to point out). He crossed Saint Joseph Lake to Holy Cross House, an assisted living facility for retired priests on the edge of campus. He might have complained a little when the staff told him that he could no longer smoke his favorite cigars inside the new building. It wasn't long before a generous donor had a small smoking shed built adjacent to the facility—heated, to help Hesburgh get through the long South Bend winters.

As he entered into his nineties, Hesburgh became the oldest living member of the US Province of Holy Cross priests and brothers. His longevity meant that he had to say goodbye to one good friend after another, both in the community and outside of it. Advanced arthritis forced Helen Hosinski, the "extraordinary woman" who served as Hesburgh's personal secretary for almost forty years, to retire in 1990. As her health deteriorated, Hesburgh visited her often in the hospital and presided at her funeral in 2000. In 2002, he was called to the bedside of another friend, Eppie Lederer, author of the syndicated "Ask Ann Landers" column. The two had known each other for over fifty years and enjoyed a special relationship (for example, they affectionately signed letters, "L. but no K."—*Love but no Kisses*). Lederer, suffering the final stages of multiple myeloma, was in excruciating pain. Though he knew his friend was Jewish, Hesburgh gave her a rosary "so that at least there's something physical you can hang on to."[26]

No loss, however, was felt as deeply as the death of Ned Joyce in 2004. Father Ted and Father Ned had worked together like the left and right hands for five decades building Notre Dame into a great Catholic university. "He has been a good half of my life and probably more," Hesburgh eulogized. "I was so close to him as a dear friend and confidant, I went to confession to him several times a year. And he didn't spare the penance. I used to laugh because I felt he knew all of my faults, probably better than I did. It was that kind of relationship."

Hesburgh later recalled climbing the steps to the pulpit to pay tribute to his friend, praying, "Lord, I don't know what I'm going to say, but I hope you'll keep me down below fifteen minutes." Without notes, Hesburgh spoke from the heart about a good priest, a trusted partner, and a beautiful human being. He concluded, "I guess all we can say is, Ned, we'll be seeing you. I truly believe that. There will be more days when we can get around and talk about the glories of this wonderful place and all the wonderful people. There will be days ahead when we can look back and thank God we got through without too many scrapes and bruises. But especially, I think we'll look back with great gratitude for that wonderful grace Jesus gave us both in making us priests."[27]

At the Jubilee Mass celebrating his first fifty years as a priest, Hesburgh returned to the guiding theme of his life, preaching about the one great mediator—the great high priest—Jesus Christ. At the heart of his own priesthood, he told those gathered in Sacred Heart Basilica, "one must remember that we have that single mediator, that single divine person with a human nature, who stood between us and God." That is what priesthood means—to be a mediator, "to stand between God and humanity, to bring humanity to God and God to humanity." That is the great grace of ordination—not an indelible mark that opens up a gulf between priest and people, but rather an unmerited gift that enables the priest to bridge the divides that separate us from God and from one another. Moreover, this gift does not belong to the ordained alone, but to all those who share the name Christian. In words that could have come from the dissertation on the laity he had written half a century earlier, Hesburgh told the assembly, "every one of you who have been baptized have been marked with the priesthood of Christ. . . . You have been empowered, not just to grow in Christ through the liturgy and all the graces of the sacraments and of daily life, but you've been empowered to go out and to speak to Christ. You've been empowered to go out and to image him to the rest of humanity. . . . We have only one priest, but we all share his priesthood."[28]

Hesburgh concluded his fiftieth-anniversary homily by returning to his own life as a priest, expressing his profound gratitude, and asking the good Lord for one last grace, namely, "to offer the holy sacrifice of the Mass every day of my life until I die. If that happens, then I'll die happy."

On February 26, 2015, sitting in a wheelchair in the chapel of Holy Cross House, Father Theodore M. Hesburgh, CSC, celebrated Mass for the last time. Throughout the day, family members, fellow priests, and old friends visited his room and sat with the dying priest as his breathing grew more labored. That night, Amivi Gbologan, the devoted nurse's aide who cared for Hesburgh in his final months, kept vigil. A native of French-speaking Togo in West Africa, Gbologan recited the rosary with "the loving father" in French. When Hesburgh asked her what was next, she replied simply, "time to close your eyes and open them in heaven."[29] He died around 11:30 p.m., two months before his ninety-eighth birthday.

In the days that followed, more than twelve thousand people passed through campus to pay their respects and to honor the legacy of a faithful priest, a visionary president, and a dedicated public servant. Hundreds of Notre Dame students stood in the cold, lining the route from Sacred Heart Basilica to the cemetery where Hesburgh would be laid to rest. Dozens of dignitaries attended his memorial. But perhaps the most moving tribute of all were those final words of Amivi Gbologan. Hesburgh had spent his life working to span the divide that separated clergy and laity, women and men, black and white, developed nations and developing nations. How appropriate that his death would bring all these together, as this lay woman from Africa helped Father Ted cross one last bridge.

Notes

Preface—pages ix–xi

1. Wilson D. Miscamble, *American Priest: The Ambitious Life and Conflicted Legacy of Notre Dame's Father Ted Hesburgh* (New York: Image, 2019), 378.

2. *Hesburgh*, directed by Patrick Creadon (Music Box Films, 2019), DVD.

Introduction—pages 1–7

1. From the introduction of Father Theodore Hesburgh on the occasion of his delivering the Terry Lectures at Yale University. See Kingman Brewster, Jr., "Preface," *The Humane Imperative: A Challenge for the Year 2000*, by Theodore M. Hesburgh (New Haven: Yale University Press, 1974), ix–xi, at xi.

2. Nathan O. Hatch, "What I Learned from Fr. Ted Hesburgh," *National Catholic Reporter*, March 5, 2015, at https://www.ncronline.org/news/people/what-i-learned-fr-ted-hesburgh.

3. Theodore M. Hesburgh, with Jerry Reedy, *God, Country, Notre Dame* (New York: Doubleday, 1990), xi. Permission requested from Notre Dame Press.

4. Hesburgh, *God, Country, Notre Dame*, x.

5. Hatch, "What I Learned from Fr. Ted Hesburgh."

Chapter One:
Faith in the Family—pages 9–20

1. Robert Cross, "Priest, College President, Citizen of the World," *Chicago Tribune*, November 12, 1978, F30.

2. Theodore M. Hesburgh, with Jerry Reedy, *God, Country, Notre Dame* (New York: Doubleday, 1990), 8.

3. Walter R. Collins, "Growing Up Ted," *Notre Dame Magazine*, Special Edition (March 2015), 8–13, at 9.

4. Michael O'Brien, *Hesburgh: A Biography* (Washington, DC: Catholic University of America Press, 1998), 7. Reprinted with permission from The Catholic University of America Press.

5. Hesburgh, *God, Country, Notre Dame*, 9.

6. Hesburgh, *God, Country, Notre Dame*, 6.

7. O'Brien, *Hesburgh: A Biography*, 7.

8. O'Brien, *Hesburgh: A Biography*, 16.

9. O'Brien, *Hesburgh: A Biography*, 17.

10. O'Brien, *Hesburgh: A Biography*, 18–19.

11. Hesburgh, *God, Country, Notre Dame*, 7.

12. David O'Brien, *Faith and Friendship: Catholicism in the Diocese of Syracuse 1886–1986* (Syracuse, NY: Catholic Diocese of Syracuse, 1987), 199, 201.

13. O'Brien, *Hesburgh: A Biography*, 9.

14. Hesburgh, *God, Country, Notre Dame*, 190.

15. O'Brien, *Faith and Friendship*, 201. For historical background on the American Catholic subculture, see William M. Halsey, *The Survival of American Innocence: Catholicism in an Era of Disillusionment, 1920–1940* (Notre Dame, IN: University of Notre Dame Press, 1980).

16. O'Brien, *Hesburgh: A Biography*, 10.

17. O'Brien, *Hesburgh: A Biography*, 11.

18. O'Brien, *Hesburgh: A Biography*, 17.

19. Hesburgh, *God, Country, Notre Dame*, 9.

20. Hesburgh, *God, Country, Notre Dame*, 14.

21. Hesburgh, *God, Country, Notre Dame*, 15.

22. O'Brien, *Hesburgh: A Biography*, 23.

23. Thomas McNally, "Moreau Seminary," *Notre Dame Scholastic* 99, no. 3 (October 11, 1957): 18–19, 22–23, at 23.

24. Hesburgh, *God, Country, Notre Dame*, 24–25.

25. Hesburgh, *God, Country, Notre Dame*, xi–xii.

26. Hesburgh, *God, Country, Notre Dame*, 26.

27. Hesburgh, *God, Country, Notre Dame*, xii.

Chapter Two:
Becoming a Theologian—pages 21–38

1. Theodore M. Hesburgh, with Jerry Reedy, *God, Country, Notre Dame* (New York: Doubleday, 1990), 27.

2. Hesburgh, *God, Country, Notre Dame*, 31.

3. Hesburgh, *God, Country, Notre Dame*, 30.

4. Eugene Patterson, "Champion for Good," *Notre Dame Magazine*, Special Edition (March 2015), 48–53, at 51.

5. Hesburgh, *God, Country, Notre Dame*, 33.

6. Hesburgh, *God, Country, Notre Dame*, 33.

7. Hesburgh, *God, Country, Notre Dame*, 33.

8. Theodore M. Hesburgh to Gabriel Cardinal Garrone, May 17, 1971, 3, Theodore M. Hesburgh Papers: Manuscripts (CPHS) 98/11, University of Notre Dame Archives (UNDA).

9. Hesburgh, *God, Country, Notre Dame*, 33.

10. Hesburgh, *God, Country, Notre Dame*, 34.

11. Hesburgh, *God, Country, Notre Dame*, 35.

12. Theodore M. Hesburgh, "Homily on the Occasion of Inauguration of John VanWovlear," n.d., 2, CPHS 141/01.03, UNDA.

13. Hesburgh, "Homily on the Occasion of Inauguration of John VanWovlear," 3.

14. Hesburgh, "Homily on the Occasion of Inauguration of John VanWovlear," 4.

15. Michael O'Brien, *Hesburgh: A Biography* (Washington, DC: Catholic University of America Press, 1998), 219.

16. O'Brien, *Hesburgh: A Biography*, 221.

17. Hesburgh, *God, Country, Notre Dame*, 42.

18. Hesburgh, *God, Country, Notre Dame*.

19. Hesburgh, *God, Country, Notre Dame*, 42 (italics in original).

20. Hesburgh, *God, Country, Notre Dame*, 40.

21. Theodore M. Hesburgh, *Letters to Service Women* (Washington, DC: National Catholic Community Service, 1952), 9, 10–11.

22. O'Brien, *Hesburgh: A Biography*, 31.

23. O'Brien, *Hesburgh: A Biography*, 32.

24. O'Brien, *Hesburgh: A Biography*, 232.

25. O'Brien, *Hesburgh: A Biography*, 233.

26. Hesburgh, *God, Country, Notre Dame*, 45.

27. Theodore M. Hesburgh, *The Theology of Catholic Action* (Notre Dame, IN: Ave Maria Press, 1946), 3–4.

28. Theodore M. Hesburgh to Thomas Steiner, May 6, 1945, Correspondence 1945–1947, Congregation of Holy Cross Indiana Province Records (CUIP), 99-H, UNDA.

29. O'Brien, *Hesburgh: A Biography*, 38–39.

30. Hesburgh, *God, Country, Notre Dame*, 52.

31. Hesburgh, *God, Country, Notre Dame*, 46–47.

32. Theodore M. Hesburgh, *God and the World of Man* (Notre Dame, IN: University of Notre Dame Press, 1950), 6.

Chapter Three:
The Pursuit of Excellence—pages 39–57

1. Theodore M. Hesburgh, with Jerry Reedy, *God, Country, Notre Dame* (New York: Doubleday, 1990), 60.

2. Hesburgh, *God, Country, Notre Dame*, 60–61.

3. "Father Theodore Hesburgh of Notre Dame dies at age 97," Obituary prepared by the University of Notre Dame Office of Media Relations, February 27, 2015, at https://hesburgh.nd.edu/for-the -media/.

4. Hesburgh, *God, Country, Notre Dame*, 64.

5. Theodore M. Hesburgh, "Wisdom and Education (1952)," in *Patterns for Educational Growth* (Notre Dame, IN: University of Notre Dame, 1958), 1–9, at 8 and 6.

6. Theodore M. Hesburgh, "The Function of Theology in the University," n.d., probably 1950, 9, Theodore M. Hesburgh Papers: Manuscripts (CPHS), 141/01, University of Notre Dame Archives (UNDA).

7. Theodore M. Hesburgh, "The Mission of a Catholic University (1954)," in *Patterns for Educational Growth* (Notre Dame, IN: University of Notre Dame Press, 1958), 21–32, at 26 and 31.

8. "Curriculum of a Catholic Liberal Arts College: A Report on the College of Arts and Letters at the UND," 1953, 2–5, Notre Dame Printed and Reference Material Dropfiles (PNDP), 91-Ar-1, UNDA.

9. Hesburgh, "The Function of Theology in the University," 11.

10. Hesburgh, *God, Country, Notre Dame*, 58.

11. Michael O'Brien, *Hesburgh: A Biography* (Washington, DC: Catholic University of America Press, 1998), 51.

12. Hesburgh, *God, Country, Notre Dame*, 67.

13. Richard Conklin, "The Maker of Notre Dame," *Notre Dame Magazine*, Special Edition (March 2015), 14–22, at 15.

14. Hesburgh, *God, Country, Notre Dame*, 77.

15. Hesburgh, *God, Country, Notre Dame*, 78.

16. Hesburgh, *God, Country, Notre Dame*, 85.

17. Leon Jaroff, "Surrender at Notre Dame," *Sports Illustrated*, January 5, 1959, 15.

18. Theodore M. Hesburgh, "The Facts of the Matter," *Sports Illustrated*, January 19, 1959, 16–17, at 17.

19. O'Brien, *Hesburgh: A Biography*, 69.

20. "Hustler for Quality," *Time*, May 7, 1956, 79.

21. O'Brien, *Hesburgh: A Biography*, 70.

22. O'Brien, *Hesburgh: A Biography*, 261.

23. Hesburgh, *God, Country, Notre Dame*, 72–73.

24. Hesburgh, *God, Country, Notre Dame*, 73.

25. Hesburgh, *God, Country, Notre Dame*, 75.

26. O'Brien, *Hesburgh: A Biography*, 70, 262.

27. "Cavanaugh Hits Mental 'Mediocrity,'" *Washington Post*, December 16, 1957, 1. See Notre Dame Foundation 1953–59: Cavanaugh Records (UFDA) 5/29, 15/03, UNDA; Philip Gleason, *Contending with Modernity: Catholic High Education in the Twentieth Century* (New York: Oxford University Press, 1995), 406–7, n. 49.

28. Theodore M. Hesburgh, "Catholic Higher Education in Twentieth Century America," Address delivered at the 58th Annual Convention of the National Catholic Educational Association, April 4, 1961, 6, CPHS 141/16, UNDA.

29. "God and Man at Notre Dame," *Time*, February 9, 1962, 48–54, at 48.

30. "God and Man at Notre Dame," 48, 54.

31. "The Library: Planning," at https://hesburghportal.nd.edu /story-administration-library-1.

32. Hesburgh, *God, Country, Notre Dame*, 59.

33. Margaret M. Grubiak, "Visualizing the Modern Catholic University: The Original Intention of 'Touchdown Jesus' at the University of Notre Dame," *Material Religion* 6, no. 3 (2010): 336–68, at 339. See Bill Schmitt, *Words of Life: Celebrating 50 Years of the Hesburgh Library's Message, Mural, and Meaning* (Notre Dame, IN: University of Notre Dame Press, 2013).

34. Valerie Fraser, *Building the New World: Studies in the Modern Architecture of Latin America, 1930–1960* (London: Verso, 2000), 62.

35. Grubiak, "Visualizing the Modern Catholic University," 356–57.

36. Grubiak, "Visualizing the Modern Catholic University," 358.

37. Grubiak, "Visualizing the Modern Catholic University," 360.

Chapter Four:
Serving the World—pages 58–80

1. Michael O'Brien, *Hesburgh: A Biography* (Washington, DC: Catholic University of America Press, 1998), 162.

2. Colman McCarthy, "Father Hesburgh: Idealist Thriving in a Rough Era," *Los Angeles Times*, November 14, 1979, E7.

3. O'Brien, *Hesburgh: A Biography*, 72.

4. Harris Wofford, *Of Kennedys and Kings: Making Sense of the Sixties* (Pittsburgh: University of Pittsburgh Press, 1992), 463.

5. Wofford, *Of Kennedys and Kings*, 478.

6. Wofford, *Of Kennedys and Kings*, 463–64.

7. O'Brien, *Hesburgh: A Biography*, 72–73.

8. Foster Rhea Dulles, *The Civil Rights Commission: 1957–1965* (East Lansing, MI: Michigan State University Press, 1968), 33.

9. Dulles, *The Civil Rights Commission*, 39.

10. Dulles, *The Civil Rights Commission*, 39.

11. Theodore M. Hesburgh, with Jerry Reedy, *God, Country, Notre Dame* (New York: Doubleday, 1990), 199.

12. Hesburgh, *God, Country, Notre Dame*, 200.

13. O'Brien, *Hesburgh: A Biography*, 75.

14. Wofford, *Of Kennedys and Kings*, 478.

15. Hesburgh, *God, Country, Notre Dame*, 200.

16. See "Dissent by Commissioner Battle," "Proposal for a Constitutional Amendment to Establish Universal Suffrage," and "Proposal to Require Equal Opportunity as a Condition of Federal Grants to Higher Education," *Report of the United States Commission on Civil Rights* (Washington, DC: US Government Printing Office, 1959), 142, 143–45, 328–29.

17. Wofford, *Of Kennedys and Kings*, 482. See Hesburgh, *God, Country, Notre Dame*, 200–201.

18. Theodore M. Hesburgh, "Address at the Civil Rights Conference sponsored by the Notre Dame Law School," February 14, 1960, 2, Theodore M. Hesburgh Papers: Manuscripts (CPHS), 141/15.03, University of Notre Dame Archives (UNDA).

19. Theodore M. Hesburgh, "Address at the Catholic Interracial Council Communion Breakfast," October 25, 1959, 1, CPHS 141/14.03, UNDA.

20. Hesburgh, "Address at the Civil Rights Conference," 3.

21. "General Statement by Commissioner Theodore M. Hesburgh," *Report of the United States Commission on Civil Rights* (Washington, DC: US Government Printing Office, 1959), 551–55, at 551.

22. Hesburgh, "Address at the Catholic Interracial Council Communion Breakfast," 9–10.

23. Hesburgh, "Address at the Catholic Interracial Council Communion Breakfast," 7–8.

24. Hesburgh, "Address at the Catholic Interracial Council Communion Breakfast," 13.

25. Theodore M. Hesburgh, "Address at the Meeting of the American Academy of Arts and Sciences," November 11, 1964, 4, CPHS 141/21.08, UNDA.

26. Eileen McNamara, *Eunice: The Kennedy Who Changed the World* (New York: Simon & Schuster, 2018), 135–37.

27. Hesburgh, *God, Country, Notre Dame*, 93.

28. Theodore Hesburgh to Sargent Shriver, March 21, 1961, CPHS 115/16, UNDA.

29. Evadna Smith Bartlett, "Volunteering for Justice and Peace," *Notre Dame Magazine*, Special Edition (March 2015), 54.

30. O'Brien, *Hesburgh: A Biography*, 88.

31. O'Brien, *Hesburgh: A Biography*, 78.

32. Theodore M. Hesburgh, "Report on Civil Rights," reprinted in *The Scholastic* 103, no. 9 (December 15, 1961): 24–26, at 24.

33. Hesburgh, "Report on Civil Rights," 25.

34. Wofford, *Of Kennedys and Kings*, 161.

35. O'Brien, *Hesburgh: A Biography*, 84. This paragraph relies on O'Brien's account.

36. Wofford, *Of Kennedys and Kings*, 420.

37. Taylor Branch, *Parting the Waters: America in the King Years, 1954–63* (New York: Simon and Schuster, 1988), 721.

38. Martin Luther King, Jr., "Letter from a Birmingham Jail," at https://kinginstitute.stanford.edu/king-papers/documents/letter -birmingham-jail.

39. Hesburgh, *God, Country, Notre Dame*, 203.

40. Hesburgh, *God, Country, Notre Dame*, 203.

41. Hesburgh, *God, Country, Notre Dame*, 206.

42. O'Brien, *Hesburgh: A Biography*, 85.

43. O'Brien, *Hesburgh: A Biography*, 85.

44. O'Brien, *Hesburgh: A Biography*, 82.

45. "General Statement by Commissioner Theodore M. Hesburgh," 553.

46. Hesburgh, *God, Country, Notre Dame*, 206.

47. Wilson D. Miscamble, *American Priest: The Ambitious Life and Conflicted Legacy of Notre Dame's Father Ted Hesburgh* (New York: Image, 2019), 269.

48. Hesburgh, *God, Country, Notre Dame*, 208.

49. O'Brien, *Hesburgh: A Biography*, 128.

50. Hesburgh, *God, Country, Notre Dame*, 209.

51. Miscamble, *American Priest*, 285.

52. Theodore M. Hesburgh, "Father Hesburgh's Program for Racial Justice," *New York Times Magazine*, October 29, 1972, 20–21, 76–83.

53. Hesburgh, *God, Country, Notre Dame*, 212.

Chapter Five:
A Catholic University—pages 81–108

1. John W. O'Malley, *What Happened at Vatican II* (Cambridge, MA: Belknap Press, 2008), 94.

2. Pope John XXIII, "Opening Speech to the Council," in *The Documents of Vatican II*, ed. Walter M. Abbott (New York: Herder and Herder, 1966), 710–19, at 718.

3. Theodore M. Hesburgh, "Catholic Higher Education in Twentieth Century America," Address delivered at the 58th Annual Convention of the National Catholic Educational Association, April 4, 1961, 5, Theodore M. Hesburgh Papers: Manuscripts (CPHS), 141/16, University of Notre Dame Archives (UNDA).

4. Theodore M. Hesburgh, "The University in the World of Change," in *Thoughts for Our Times, no. 2: More Thoughts for Our Times* (Notre Dame, IN: University of Notre Dame Press, 1964), 45–58, at 45–46.

5. Hesburgh, "Catholic Higher Education in Twentieth Century America," 3.

6. Hesburgh, "Catholic Higher Education in Twentieth Century America," 8.

7. Hesburgh, "Catholic Higher Education in Twentieth Century America," 3.

8. Susan L. Poulson and Loretta P. Higgins, "Gender, Coeducation, and the Transformation of Catholic Identity in American Catholic Higher Education," *Catholic Historical Review* 89, no. 3 (July 2003): 489–510, at 494.

9. For a powerful collection of memories by alumnae testifying to their appreciation for Hesburgh's leadership, see *Thanking Father Ted: Thirty-Five Years of Notre Dame Coeducation*, ed. Ann Therese Darin Palmer (Kansas City, MO: Andrews McMeel, 2007).

10. Theodore M. Hesburgh, with Jerry Reedy, *God, Country, Notre Dame* (New York: Doubleday, 1990), 171.

11. Hesburgh, *God, Country, Notre Dame*, 171.

12. The theologians banned—John Courtney Murray, Gustave Weigel, Godfrey Diekmann, and Hans Küng—were influential figures at the Vatican Council then underway. See Joseph Nuesse, *The*

Catholic University of America: A Centennial History (Washington, DC: Catholic University of America Press, 1990), 395.

13. On the "contagion of liberty," see Gleason, *Contending with Modernity*, 224–27.

14. "Session V, January 25, 1967," 19, in *Minutes of the Provincial Chapter 1967*, Congregation of Holy Cross Indiana Province Records (CUIP), bound volumes, UNDA.

15. Alice Gallin, *Independence and a New Partnership in Catholic Higher Education* (Notre Dame, IN: University of Notre Dame Press, 1996), 1.

16. Interview of Edmund A. Stephan, conducted by Richard W. Conklin, May 2, 1983, 7, Edmund A. Stephan Papers (CZBP), UNDA.

17. Hesburgh, *God, Country, Notre Dame*, 170.

18. "Session V, January 25, 1967," 28.

19. Notre Dame Department of Public Information Press Release, May 6, 1967, 2, Public Relations Department (PRH), 1965/5, UNDA.

20. Hesburgh, *God, Country, Notre Dame*, 229.

21. Hesburgh, *God, Country, Notre Dame*, 225.

22. David O'Brien comments that the stated focus of the discussion was not colleges but universities—research institutions—none of which had a female president at the time. Yet, the distinction was artificial, "because the institutions represented at Land O'Lakes devoted almost all of their resources to undergraduate instruction, not research." David J. O'Brien, "The Land O'Lakes Statement," *Boston College Magazine*, Winter 1998, at http://www.bc.edu/content/dam/files/offices/mission/pdf1/cu7.pdf.

23. Gleason, *Contending with Modernity*, 317.

24. "Land O'Lakes Statement: The Nature of the Contemporary Catholic University," in *American Catholic Higher Education: Essential Documents, 1967–1990*, ed. Alice Gallin (Notre Dame, IN: University of Notre Dame Press, 1992), 7–12, at 7.

25. Neil G. McCluskey, "Introduction: This is How It Happened," in *The Catholic University: A Modern Appraisal*, ed. Neil G. McClusky (Notre Dame, IN: University of Notre Dame Press, 1970), 1–28, at 7.

26. "Land O'Lakes Statement," 7.

27. "Land O'Lakes Statement," 8, 9. For a fuller treatment of Hesburgh's underlying vision, see Edward P. Hahnenberg, "Theodore M. Hesburgh, Theologian: Revisiting Land O'Lakes Fifty Years Later," *Theological Studies* 78, no. 4 (2017): 930–59.

28. Theodore M. Hesburgh, "Foreword," in *Thoughts IV: Five Addresses Delivered During 1967* (Notre Dame, IN: University of Notre Dame Press, 1968), n.p.

29. Hesburgh, "The Vision of a Great Catholic University," in *Thoughts IV*, 1–16, at 5.

30. Hesburgh, "The Vision of a Great Catholic University," 9, 8.

31. Hesburgh, "The Vision of a Great Catholic University," 10.

32. Hesburgh, "The Vision of a Great Catholic University," 12.

33. Hesburgh, "The Vision of a Great Catholic University," 11–12.

34. Hesburgh, "The Challenge Ahead," in *Thoughts IV: Five Addresses Delivered During 1967* (Notre Dame, IN: University of Notre Dame Press, 1968), 17–28, at 21–22.

35. Theodore M. Hesburgh, "The 'Events': A Retrospective View," *Daedalus* 103, no. 4 (Fall 1974): 66–71, at 68.

36. Michael O'Brien, *Hesburgh: A Biography* (Washington, DC: Catholic University of America Press, 1998), 94.

37. Joel R. Connelly and Howard J. Dooley, *Hesburgh's Notre Dame: Triumph in Transition* (New York: Hawthorn Books, 1972), 42.

38. "Why Not 'Chancellor' Hesburgh?," *Scholastic* 104, no. 13 (February 22, 1963): 7.

39. Wilson D. Miscamble, *American Priest: The Ambitious Life and Conflicted Legacy of Notre Dame's Father Ted Hesburgh* (New York: Image, 2019), 94.

40. Connelly and Dooley, *Hesburgh's Notre Dame*, 56, 57.

41. Theodore M. Hesburgh, "This New Generation," *America* 109, no. 14 (October 5, 1963): 385.

42. "Versatile Ecumenist: Theodore Martin Hesburgh," *New York Times*, October 10, 1967, 35.

43. Hesburgh, "The 'Events,' " 68.

44. Hesburgh, *God, Country, Notre Dame*, 108.

45. Richard Rossie, Notre Dame student body president 1968–69, cited in O'Brien, *Hesburgh: A Biography*, 101.

46. Connelly and Dooley, *Hesburgh's Notre Dame*, 250.

47. "Blacks Demonstrate at Game," *The Observer* 3, no. 50 (November 18, 1968), 2. See Miscamble, *American Priest*, 131.

48. "Hesburgh Hits CIA Lie-In," *The Observer* 3, no. 55 (November 25, 1968), 1.

49. O'Brien, *Hesburgh: A Biography*, 105.

50. Theodore M. Hesburgh to Notre Dame Faculty and Students, February 17, 1969, 1–2, Notre Dame Printed and Reference Material (PNDP), 30-Pr-f2, UNDA. Cited in Hesburgh, *God, Country, Notre Dame*, 113–18, at 114.

51. Hesburgh, *God, Country, Notre Dame*, 117.

52. Hesburgh, *God, Country, Notre Dame*, 115.

53. Hesburgh, *God, Country, Notre Dame*, 113.

54. Hesburgh, *God, Country, Notre Dame*, 130.

55. Margaret Fosmoe, "Fifteen Minutes, 50 Years Later," *Notre Dame Magazine* (Winter 2019–20), at http://magazine.nd.edu/stories/fifteen-minutes-50-years-later/.

56. Hesburgh, *God, Country, Notre Dame*, 113.

57. Hesburgh, *God, Country, Notre Dame*, 119.

58. Hesburgh, *God, Country, Notre Dame*, 107.

59. O'Brien, *Hesburgh: A Biography*, 116.

60. O'Brien, *Hesburgh: A Biography*, 114.

61. Robert Schmuhl, "Seven Days in May," *Notre Dame Magazine* 18, no. 4 (Winter 1989–90), 22–25, at 25.

62. O'Brien, *Hesburgh: A Biography*, 114. See Mark Walbran, "Christian Peace, Love at Resistance Mass," *The Observer* 4, no. 23 (October 16, 1969), 2

63. Hesburgh, *God, Country, Notre Dame*, 108–9.

64. "Hesburgh Condemns Nixon," *The Observer* 4, no. 122 (May 5, 1970), 1.

65. "Statement Text," *The Observer* 4, no. 122 (May 5, 1970), 1.

66. This paragraph draws heavily on O'Brien, *Hesburgh: A Biography*, 118–22.

67. O'Brien, *Hesburgh: A Biography*, 115.

68. Hesburgh, "The 'Events,'" 70–71.

Chapter Six:
The Humane Imperative—pages 109–33

1. Theodore M. Hesburgh, *The Humane Imperative: A Challenge for the Year 2000* (New Haven: Yale University Press, 1974), 1.

2. Hesburgh, *The Humane Imperative*, 103.

3. Michael O'Brien, *Hesburgh: A Biography* (Washington, DC: Catholic University of America Press, 1998), 145.

4. O'Brien, *Hesburgh: A Biography*, 145–46.

5. Theodore M. Hesburgh, "Problems and Opportunities on a Very Interdependent Planet," in *The Hesburgh Papers: Higher Values in Higher Education* (Kansas City, MO: Andrews & McMeel, 1979), 196–206, at 200.

6. Robert Cross, "Priest, College President, Citizen of the World," *Chicago Tribune*, November 12, 1978, F30. Cited in O'Brien, *Hesburgh: A Biography*, 148.

7. Hesburgh, "Problems and Opportunities on a Very Interdependent Planet," 201.

8. Hesburgh, "Problems and Opportunities on a Very Interdependent Planet," 200.

9. Hesburgh, *The Humane Imperative*, 50.

10. Donald T. Critchlow, *Intended Consequences: Birth Control, Abortion, and the Federal Government in Modern America* (New York: Oxford University Press, 1999), 13.

11. Critchlow, *Intended Consequences*, 54–56.

12. Critchlow, *Intended Consequences*, 19–29.

13. Wilson D. Miscamble, *American Priest: The Ambitious Life and Conflicted Legacy of Notre Dame's Father Ted Hesburgh* (New York: Image, 2019), 215.

14. Theodore M. Hesburgh, "The Christian Family," January 21, 1947, 1–2, Theodore M. Hesburgh Papers: Manuscripts (CPHS), 141/01.01, University of Notre Dame Archives (UNDA).

15. John Wicklein, "U.S. Study Asked on Birth Control," *New York Times*, January 15, 1960, 7.

16. O'Brien, *Hesburgh: A Biography*, 142.

17. O'Brien, *Hesburgh: A Biography*, 248–49.

18. See Thomas E. Blantz, *George N. Shuster: On the Side of Truth* (Notre Dame, IN: University of Notre Dame Press, 1993), 314–24.

19. Stephen R. Schloesser, "'*Dancing on the Edge of the Volcano*': Biopolitics and What Happened after Vatican II," in *From Vatican II to Pope Francis: Charting a Catholic Future*, ed. Paul Crowley (Maryknoll, NY: Orbis Books, 2014), 3–26, at 7–8. See Mark Kurlansky, *1968: The Year That Rocked the World* (New York: Ballantine, 2004).

20. Richard Conklin, "The Maker of Notre Dame," *Notre Dame Magazine*, Special Edition (March 2015), 14–22, at 18.

21. O'Brien, *Hesburgh: A Biography*, 287.

22. Miscamble, *American Priest*, 256.

23. Theodore M. Hesburgh, with Jerry Reedy, *God, Country, Notre Dame* (New York: Doubleday, 1990), 262.

24. Hesburgh, *God, Country, Notre Dame*, 258.

25. Hesburgh, *God, Country, Notre Dame*, 263–64.

26. Hesburgh, *God, Country, Notre Dame*, 266–67.

27. John C. Lungren, *Hesburgh of Notre Dame: Priest, Educator, Public Servant* (Kansas City, MO: Sheed & Ward, 1987), 87.

28. Hesburgh, *God, Country, Notre Dame*, 268.

29. Hesburgh, *God, Country, Notre Dame*, 271.

30. Miscamble, *American Priest*, 302.

31. Hesburgh, *The Humane Imperative*, 33. See Miscamble, *American Priest*, 154.

32. O'Brien, *Hesburgh: A Biography*, 254.

33. Kenneth L. Woodward, "History or Hit Job? An Unflattering Bio of Fr. Ted Hesburgh," *Commonweal* 146, no. 10 (June 1, 2019): 16–20, at 18.

34. Miscamble, *American Priest*, 154.

35. Theodore M. Hesburgh, Address at the National Convention of the Catholic Press Association, April 24, 1974, 15. CPHS 142/07.03, UNDA.

36. Theodore M. Hesburgh, "Reflections on Cuomo: The Secret Consensus," *Notre Dame Journal of Law, Ethics & Public Policy* 1, no. 1 (1985): 53–56, at 54 and 56.

37. "The Foundations of Foreign Policy: President Carter's Commencement Address at the University of Notre Dame," Commence-

ment 1977, May 22, 1977, Notre Dame Information Services (UDIS), 61/18, UNDA.

38. Theodore M. Hesburgh, "The Priest as Mediator and Ambassador," in *Between God and Caesar: Priests, Sisters and Political Office in the United States*, ed. Madonna Kolbenschlag (Mahwah and New York: Paulist Press, 1985), 282–90.

39. Hesburgh, *God, Country, Notre Dame*, 276.

40. Miscamble, *American Priest*, 312.

41. The previous two paragraphs rely on O'Brien, *Hesburgh: A Biography*, 151–56.

42. Miscamble, *American Priest*, 315.

43. Theodore M. Hesburgh, "Foreword," *Catholics and Nuclear War: A Commentary on the Challenge of Peace*, ed. Philip J. Murnion (New York: Crossroad, 1983), vii–xiii, at xii.

44. Recounted in Miscamble, *American Priest*, 181–82.

45. O'Brien, *Hesburgh: A Biography*, 173.

46. O'Brien, *Hesburgh: A Biography*, 170.

47. O'Brien, *Hesburgh: A Biography*, 169.

48. Colman McCarthy, "Father Hesburgh: Idealist Thriving in a Rough Era," *Los Angeles Times* (November 14, 1979), E7.

49. O'Brien, *Hesburgh: A Biography*, 162.

Chapter Seven:
To the End—pages 134–50

1. Theodore M. Hesburgh, with Jerry Reedy, *God, Country, Notre Dame* (New York: Doubleday, 1990), 304.

2. Michael O'Brien, *Hesburgh: A Biography* (Washington, DC: Catholic University of America Press, 1998), 296.

3. Theodore M. Hesburgh, *Travels with Ted & Ned*, ed. Jerry Reedy (New York: Doubleday, 1992), 3.

4. O'Brien, *Hesburgh: A Biography*, 297.

5. Hesburgh, *God, Country, Notre Dame*, 304.

6. Hesburgh, *God, Country, Notre Dame*, 305.

7. O'Brien, *Hesburgh: A Biography*, 311.

8. O'Brien, *Hesburgh: A Biography*, 298.

9. O'Brien, *Hesburgh: A Biography*, 304.

10. Wilson D. Miscamble, *American Priest: The Ambitious Life and Conflicted Legacy of Notre Dame's Father Ted Hesburgh* (New York: Image, 2019), 353. This section relies on Miscamble's account.

11. Robert Schmuhl, *Fifty Years with Father Hesburgh: On and Off the Record* (Notre Dame, IN: University of Notre Dame Press, 2016), 117–18.

12. Theodore M. Hesburgh, "If I Had Five Minutes with the Pope," *America* 157, no. 6 (September 19, 1987): 129–30.

13. Theodore M. Hesburgh, "Where Are College Presidents' Voices on Important Public Issues?," *Chronicle of Higher Education* 47, no. 21 (February 2, 2001): 20.

14. "Seen & Heard," *Notre Dame Magazine* (Summer 2013), 17.

15. John Nagy, "His National Birthday Party," *Notre Dame Magazine*, Special Edition (March 2015), 78–79.

16. "Obama's Commencement Address at Notre Dame," *New York Times*, May 17, 2009.

17. Theodore M. Hesburgh, letter to the editor, *Notre Dame Magazine* (Fall 2009), 3.

18. President William J. Clinton, "Remarks on Presenting the Congressional Gold Medal to Father Theodore M. Hesburgh," July 13, 2000, at https://www.govinfo.gov/content/pkg/PPP-2000-book2/pdf/PPP-2000-book2-doc-pg1424.pdf.

19. Hesburgh, *God, Country, Notre Dame*, ix.

20. Miscamble, *American Priest*, 144.

21. John Salveson, "I Was Abused . . . and 25 Years Later I'm Still Trying to Make Things Right," *Notre Dame Magazine* 32, no. 2 (Summer 2003), 24–29, at 29.

22. Salveson, "I Was Abused," 29.

23. Hesburgh, *God, Country, Notre Dame*, 311, 313.

24. O'Brien, *Hesburgh: A Biography*, 310.

25. Schmuhl, *Fifty Years with Father Hesburgh*, 110.

26. Carol Felsenthal, "Father Hesburgh and His Close Friendship with Ann Landers," *Chicago Magazine*, February 28, 2015, at https://www.chicagomag.com/Chicago-Magazine/Felsenthal-Files/February-2015/Fr-Hesburgh/.

27. Theodore M. Hesburgh, "Goodbye, Friend: A Homily for Father Joyce," May 5, 2004, at https://news.nd.edu/news/goodbye -friend-a-homily-for-father-joyce/.

28. Theodore M. Hesburgh, "50th Anniversary Mass," May 6, 1993, at https://hesburghportal.nd.edu/media.

29. *Hesburgh*, directed by Patrick Creadon (Music Box Films, 2019), DVD.

Bibliography

Primary Sources by Theodore M. Hesburgh

Published Materials

"The 'Events': A Retrospective View." *Daedalus* 103, no. 4 (Fall 1974): 66–71.

"Father Hesburgh's Program for Racial Justice." *New York Times Magazine.* October 29, 1972.

"Fiftieth Anniversary Mass." *Father Hesburgh's Life & Legacy.* May 6, 1993. Video, 26:42. https://hesburghportal.nd.edu /media.

"General Statement by Commissioner Theodore M. Hesburgh." In *Report of the United States Commission on Civil Rights,* 551–55. Washington, DC: US Government Printing Office, 1959.

God and the World of Man. Notre Dame, IN: University of Notre Dame Press, 1950.

God, Country, Notre Dame (with Jerry Reedy). New York: Doubleday, 1990.

"Goodbye, Friend: A Homily for Father Joyce." May 5, 2004. https://news.nd.edu/news/goodbye-friend-a-homily-for -father-joyce/.

The Hesburgh Papers: Higher Values in Higher Education. Kansas City, MO: Andrews & McMeel, 1979.

The Humane Imperative: A Challenge for the Year 2000. New Haven: Yale University Press, 1974.

"If I Had Five Minutes with the Pope." *America* 157, no. 6 (September 19, 1987): 129–30.

Letters to Service Women. Washington, DC: National Catholic Community Service, 1952.

Patterns for Educational Growth. Notre Dame, IN: University of Notre Dame Press, 1958.

"The Priest as Mediator and Ambassador." In *Between God and Caesar: Priests, Sisters and Political Office in the United States,* edited by Madonna Kolbenschlag. New York and Mahwah: Paulist Press, 1985.

"Reflections on Cuomo: The Secret Consensus." *Notre Dame Journal of Law, Ethics & Public Policy* 1, no. 1 (1985): 53–56.

"Report on Civil Rights." Reprinted in *The Scholastic* 103, no. 9 (December 15, 1961): 24–26.

The Theology of Catholic Action. Notre Dame, IN: Ave Maria Press, 1946.

"This New Generation." *America* 109, no. 14 (October 5, 1963): 385.

Thoughts for Our Times, no. 1. Notre Dame, IN: University of Notre Dame Press, 1962.

Thoughts for Our Times, no. 2: *More Thoughts for Our Times.* Notre Dame, IN: University of Notre Dame Press, 1964.

Thoughts for Our Times, no. 3: *Still More Thoughts for Our Times.* Notre Dame, IN: University of Notre Dame Press, 1966.

Thoughts for Our Times, no. 4: *Thoughts IV. Five Addresses Delivered During 1967.* Notre Dame, IN: University of Notre Dame Press, 1967.

Thoughts for Our Times, no. 5: *Thoughts for Our Times V.* Notre Dame, IN: University of Notre Dame Press, 1969.

Three Bicentennial Addresses. Notre Dame, IN: University of Notre Dame Press, 1976.

Travels with Ted & Ned, edited by Jerry Reedy (New York: Doubleday, 1992).

"Where Are College Presidents' Voices on Important Public Issues?" *Chronicle of Higher Education* 47, no. 21 (February 2, 2001): B20.

"The Work of Mediation." *Commonweal* 75, no. 2 (October 6, 1961): 33–35.

Unpublished Speeches

"Address at the Annual Convention of the National Federation of Priests' Councils." March 15, 1971. CPHS 142/04.02. UNDA.

"Address at the Catholic Interracial Council Communion Breakfast." October 25, 1959. Theodore M. Hesburgh Papers: Manuscripts (CPHS) 141/14.03. University of Notre Dame Archives (UNDA).

"Address at the Civil Rights Conference sponsored by the Notre Dame Law School." February 14, 1960. CPHS 141/15.03. UNDA.

"Address at the Meeting of the American Academy of Arts and Sciences." November 11, 1964. CPHS 141/21.08. UNDA.

"Address at the National Convention of the Catholic Press Association." April 24, 1974, 15. CPHS 142/07.03. UNDA.

"Catholic Higher Education in Twentieth Century America." Address delivered at the 58th Annual Convention of the National Catholic Educational Association, April 4, 1961. CPHS 141/16. UNDA.

"The Character of a Christian." July 13, 1951. CPHS 141/02.01. UNDA.

"The Christian Family." January 21, 1947. CPHS 141/01.01. UNDA.

"The Function of Theology in the University," n.d., probably 1950. CPHS 141/01. UNDA.

"Homily on the Occasion of Inauguration of John VanWovlear," n.d. CPHS 141/01.03. UNDA.

Secondary Sources

Ames, Charlotte A. *Theodore M. Hesburgh: A Bio-Bibliography*. New York: Greenwood Press, 1989.

Blantz, Thomas E. *George N. Shuster: On the Side of Truth*. Notre Dame, IN: University of Notre Dame Press, 1993.

Clinton, William J. "Remarks on Presenting the Congressional Gold Medal to Father Theodore M. Hesburgh." July 13, 2000. https://www.govinfo.gov/content/pkg/PPP-2000 -book2/pdf/PPP-2000-book2-doc-pg1424.pdf.

Connelly, Joel R., and Howard J. Dooley. *Hesburgh's Notre Dame: Triumph in Transition*. New York: Hawthorn Books, 1972.

Creadon, Patrick, director. *Hesburgh*. Music Box Films, 2019. DVD.

Critchlow, Donald T. *Intended Consequences: Birth Control, Abortion, and the Federal Government in Modern America*. New York: Oxford University Press, 1999.

Cross, Robert. "Priest, College President, Citizen of the World." *Chicago Tribune*, November 12, 1978.

Darin Palmer, Ann Therese, ed. *Thanking Father Ted: Thirty-Five Years of Notre Dame Coeducation*. Kansas City, MO: Andrews McMeel, 2007.

Dulles, Foster Rhea. *The Civil Rights Commission: 1957–1965*. East Lansing, MI: Michigan State University Press, 1968.

"Father Theodore Hesburgh of Notre Dame dies at age 97." Obituary prepared by the University of Notre Dame Office of Media Relations. February 27, 2015. https://hesburgh .nd.edu/for-the-media/.

Felsenthal, Carol. "Father Hesburgh and His Close Friendship with Ann Landers." *Chicago Magazine*, February 28, 2015. https://www.chicagomag.com/Chicago-Magazine /Felsenthal-Files/February-2015/Fr-Hesburgh/.

Fosmoe, Margaret. "Fifteen Minutes, 50 Years Later." *Notre Dame Magazine*, Winter 2019–20. http://magazine.nd.edu /stories/fifteen-minutes-50-years-later/.

Gallin, Alice, ed. *American Catholic Higher Education: Essential Documents, 1967–1990*. Notre Dame, IN: University of Notre Dame Press, 1992.

———. *Independence and a New Partnership in Catholic Higher Education*. Notre Dame, IN: University of Notre Dame Press, 1996.

———. *Negotiating Identity: Catholic Higher Education Since 1960*. Notre Dame, IN: University of Notre Dame Press, 2000.

Gleason, Philip. *Contending with Modernity: Catholic Higher Education in the Twentieth Century*. New York: Oxford University Press, 1995.

"God and Man at Notre Dame." *Time* (cover story), February 9, 1962.

Grubiak, Margaret M. "Visualizing the Modern Catholic University: The Original Intention of 'Touchdown Jesus' at the University of Notre Dame." *Material Religion* 6, no. 3 (2010): 336–68.

Hahnenberg, Edward P. "Theodore M. Hesburgh, Theologian: Revisiting Land O'Lakes Fifty Years Later." *Theological Studies* 78, no. 4 (2017): 930–59.

Hatch, Nathan O. "What I Learned from Fr. Ted Hesburgh." *National Catholic Reporter*, March 5, 2015. https://www.ncronline.org/news/people/what-i-learned-fr-ted-hesburgh.

Hogan, Mary Patience. "Father Theodore M. Hesburgh and the University of Notre Dame's Change in Governance to a Predominantly Lay Board of Trustees." PhD dissertation, Seton Hall University, 2009.

Horton, Thomas R. "Theodore M. Hesburgh, C.S.C." In *"What Works for Me": 16 CEOs Talk About Their Careers and Commitments*. New York: Random House, 1986.

"Hustler for Quality." *Time*, May 7, 1956.

Lungren, John C. *Hesburgh of Notre Dame: Priest, Educator, Public Servant*. Kansas City, MO: Sheed & Ward, 1987.

McCarthy, Colman. "Father Hesburgh: Idealist Thriving in a Rough Era." *Los Angeles Times*, November 14, 1979.

McCluskey, Neil G., ed. *The Catholic University: A Modern Appraisal.* Notre Dame, IN: University of Notre Dame Press, 1970.

Miscamble, Wilson D. *American Priest: The Ambitious Life and Conflicted Legacy of Notre Dame's Father Ted Hesburgh.* New York: Image, 2019.

O'Brien, David J. *Faith and Friendship: Catholicism in the Diocese of Syracuse 1886–1986.* Syracuse, NY: Catholic Diocese of Syracuse, 1987.

————. "The Land O'Lakes Statement." *Boston College Magazine,* Winter 1998. http://www.bc.edu/content/dam/files/offices /mission/pdf1/cu7.pdf.

O'Brien, Michael. *Hesburgh: A Biography.* Washington, DC: Catholic University of America Press, 1998.

Rev. Theodore M. Hesburgh, C.S.C.: Priest, President, Citizen of the World, 1917–2015. Special Edition of *Notre Dame Magazine,* March 2015.

Salveson, John. "I Was Abused . . . and 25 Years Later I'm Still Trying to Make Things Right." *Notre Dame Magazine* 32, no. 2 (Summer 2003), 24–29.

Schlereth, Thomas J. *The University of Notre Dame: A Portrait of Its History and Campus.* Notre Dame, IN: University of Notre Dame Press, 1976.

Schmitt, Bill. *Words of Life: Celebrating 50 Years of the Hesburgh Library's Message, Mural, and Meaning.* Notre Dame, IN: University of Notre Dame Press, 2013.

Schmuhl, Robert P. *Fifty Years with Father Hesburgh: On and Off the Record.* Notre Dame, IN: University of Notre Dame Press, 2016.

————. "Seven Days in May." *Notre Dame Magazine* 18, no. 4 (Winter 1989–90), 22–25.

————. *University of Notre Dame: A Contemporary Portrait.* Notre Dame, IN: University of Notre Dame Press, 1986.

Stritch, Thomas. "A Short Biography of Theodore Hesburgh." In
    Theodore M. Hesburgh: A Bio-Bibliography, edited by
    Charlotte A. Ames. New York: Greenwood Press, 1989.

"Versatile Ecumenist: Theodore Martin Hesburgh." *New York
    Times*, October 10, 1967.

Wofford, Harris. *Of Kennedys and Kings: Making Sense of the
    Sixties*. Pittsburgh: University of Pittsburgh Press, 1992.

Woodward, Kenneth L. "History or Hit Job? An Unflattering Bio
    of Fr. Ted Hesburgh." *Commonweal* 146, no. 10 (June 1,
    2019): 16–20.

Index